From the reviews of
Whose Puck Is It, Anyway?

"I wish this book was required reading for every minor hockey coach and parent."

        – Dave Dawson, *Orillia Packet and Times*

"Arnold set out to prove the radical – to some – theory that hockey, even competitive hockey, can be fun. He brings the reader on the bus, into the dressing room and behind the bench with this young team. I would recommend this book to anyone involved in minor hockey – especially those who disagree with Arnold's philosophy."

        – Ian MacAlpine, Kingston *Whig-Standard*

"*Whose Puck Is It, Anyway?* by Ed Arnold is a must for a hockey parent or coach, past, present or future. If you are a minor hockey coach or have a son or daughter in the sport, you owe it to yourself to read this book."

        – Rosalie MacEachern, *New Glasgow Evening News*

"Arnold's approach steers the focus away from past priorities such as winning, scoring and ice time and focuses on bringing fun back into the game."   – The NHL Network

"Imagine a minor hockey team being operated with the prime objective being to give boys and girls a fun winter. Coaches, commending players for good plays rather than criticizing them for mistakes. Equal ice time for all."

        – Neil Stevens, *Canadian Press*

"Arnold's coaching mandate – to have fun on the ice – is nothing new. But, it's rare for a coach at his level in the hockey system to practice it. He wants kids to enjoy the game."

– Brenda Hampton, *TV Guide*

"Everyone who cares about minor hockey should read this book."

– Bob McCowan, The FAN

"Here's a guy who ran a team where the whole premise was to have fun. He said all the things you'd want kids to experience."

– Professor Alan Leschied, *London Free Press*

"Maybe it will start a new trend." – *Truro Daily News*

"[*Whose Puck Is It, Anyway?*] could serve just as well as a how-to-book on coaching minor hockey."

– Bernd Franke, *Welland Tribune*

WHOSE PUCK IS IT, ANYWAY?

A Season with a Minor Novice Hockey Team

ED ARNOLD

M&S

Cloth edition published 2002
Trade paperback edition 2003

National Library of Canada Cataloguing in Publication

Arnold, Ed
Whose puck is it, anyway? : a season with a
minor novice hockey team / Ed Arnold.

ISBN 0-7710-0780-9 (bound).—ISBN 0-7710-0781-7 (pbk.)

1. Hockey for children–Ontario–Peterborough. I. Title.

GV848.6.C45A76 2002   796.962'6   C2002-902126-X

We acknowledge the financial support of the Government of Canada
through the Book Publishing Industry Development Program and that of
the Government of Ontario through the Ontario Media Development
Corporation's Ontario Book Initiative. We further acknowledge the support
of the Canada Council for the Arts and the Ontario Arts Council
for our publishing program.

Published simultaneously in the United States of America by
McClelland & Stewart Ltd., P.O. Box 1030, Plattsburgh, New York 12901

Library of Congress Control Number: 2002107047

Typeset in Plaintin by M&S, Toronto
Printed and bound in Canada
This book is printed on acid-free paper that is 100% ancient
forest friendly (100% post-consumer recycled)

McClelland & Stewart Ltd.
The Canadian Publishers
481 University Avenue
Toronto, Ontario
M5G 2E9
www.mcclelland.com

1   2   3   4   5   07   06   05   04   03

CONTENTS

For the kids of the minor novice Petes 2000–2001 as well as Lorna, Kim, and Scott, who know why I coached the kids. The answer stares at me from every team photo.

For those of us who have been in and around ice hockey all of our lives this eight-month journey with the AAA Novice Petes has a lot of new scenery. The words fun, fair play, improvement, equal, and rewarding replace more common hockey terms such as . . . hard work, get the edge, sacrifice, and the big one: *win*!

Ice hockey for Canadians is part of who we are. It's as natural to us as wine is to the French, as downhill skiing is to the Austrians, as business is to the Americans. Canadians grow up with an understanding of ice hockey. Everyone learns to skate. And most of us have played the game in some form, whether on the street, on a pond, or in an arena. It is also very possible that we will have fallen in love with this wonderful, exciting, fast, addictive game.

Hockey was invented in the 1890s and by 1910 it had become a professional sport. Professionalism implies two necessary and important elements: money and results. To earn money and achieve results, ideas such as, "winning at all costs"; "if you're not cheating, you're not trying"; "if you can't beat 'em in the alley you can't beat 'em on the ice"; and many others became part of ice hockey culture. We understand the sport based on this model, and we apply it to our youth hockey programs.

On a conscious level we know this isn't right, but at a deeper level we're not so sure. Can we change the model without changing the game we know, without being unfaithful to tradition, without feeling like traitors to real Canadian ice hockey?

The answer is in the book you are about to read, but be prepared to look at the game in a new way as Ed Arnold and his staff show us the courage and determination it takes to be different – and be prepared also to have some *fun*!

Ed Arnold, as those of us who know him will attest, is nobody's fool. When he set out to challenge the conventional hockey model he surrounded himself with some very capable people. Both Steve Larmer and Greg Millen are former NHL players who are still earning their living in pro hockey. They bring with them experience, knowledge, passion, and, most importantly, credibility. This is critical, but don't be thrown off track: Ed Arnold is the designer, the builder, and the caretaker of this project. He can taste it, smell it, feel it, and it works because of him.

From the first day of August tryouts the concept is placed before all the participants, the players, and, more importantly, the parents, by Ed and the staff. The vehicle is solidly built, the coaches 100 per cent committed, and the trip, through a

Canadian winter with the AAA Minor Novice Petes, proceeds on schedule. The journey takes us into the regular season, on bus trips, to practices, tournaments, and, finally, into the playoffs. It is a wonderful trip with mountains of effort, time, and commitment – both physical and emotional – invested by everyone. It is not a trip without obstacles. Problems are addressed, solutions are found, and the *team* moves on. To the end, the coaches are true to their philosophy: have fun, do our best, let the players discover the best way, give equal ice time, never yell at players or officials. Sound too good to be true? Read on!

There is another level of value and enjoyment in this journal. Through Ed Arnold's eyes and pen we are given access to the powerful attraction of team sport. The meshing together of seventeen players, parents, and staff. The caring phone calls to "see how someone is doing." The nicknames, the razzing, the joy in seeing the next guy or girl succeed. The connection is so deep that even I wonder why "Loops" (Greg Millen) would be in Vancouver to broadcast an NHL game when he should be and wants to be with the AAA Novice Petes – his *team*!

Was the concept a success? Did the AAA Novice Petes accomplish what they set out to do? *Yes!* Was it perfect? Have they restructured the face of minor hockey in Canada? Probably not, but they *have* shown us that the great things about the sport of ice hockey that we love will not disappear, and have a chance to improve if we have the guts to resist the win-at-all-costs philosophy.

But to resist it takes the maturity, the belief, the ability to sell, the determination not to retreat when things look bleak that Ed and his staff present, that the parents and kids bought into. If more coaches, parents, and league organizers join the crusade and the concept gains momentum, the rewards will multiply. If ever the concept approached mainstream, we would all wonder how we ever believed it should be different. Why did we not separate the values and needs of minor hockey and professional hockey a long time ago?

– BOB GAINEY

Bob Gainey is the former captain of the Montreal Canadiens and general manager of the Dallas Stars in the NHL. He resigned in 2002 and is now a team consultant.

THE COACHES

Ed "Teak" Arnold is the managing editor of the Peterborough *Examiner*, a daily newspaper in Peterborough, Ontario. He has coached minor hockey for eleven years, most of it at the AAA novice level. He has received numerous newspaper writing awards and has also received the Ontario Medal of Citizenship Award for his work with Peterborough children.

Steve "Coach" Larmer. A former National Hockey League player, Steve Larmer won the Calder Cup as NHL Rookie of the Year. He played thirteen years with the Chicago Blackhawks and New York Rangers from 1982 to 1995, finishing in the top twenty in goals, assists, and points in the league. Steve appeared in 884 consecutive games. During the course of his career he scored 1,012 points with 441 goals and 571 assists, playing in 1,006 regular-season games. He won a Stanley Cup championship with the New York Rangers and the Canada Cup with Team Canada in 1991. After retiring from playing hockey, he joined the National Hockey League Players' Association as an employee; he is also a member of the Canadian Hockey Association's Board of Directors. He was involved in Canada's Open Ice Hockey Summit, a conference that looked at the problems facing minor hockey in Canada.

Greg "Loops" Millen is a former National Hockey League goalie, having played with St. Louis, Chicago, Quebec, Pittsburgh, Detroit, and Hartford. Greg played fourteen years in the NHL from 1978 to 1992. He played in 1,281 games with seventeen shutouts and a 3.87 goals-against average. He also starred with the Peterborough Petes in junior hockey and makes his home near Peterborough today. Greg is a CBC hockey analyst for *Hockey Night in Canada*.

Bill Gillam, born in Corner Brook, Newfoundland, grew up in Toronto and Peterborough, where he played minor hockey. He also played for his university, Geneseo State, in the NCAA Division III, and in the East Coast and International leagues, before returning to Peterborough, where he has coached at the bantam and tyke levels.

Mayhem on the Ice

Every night in Canada during the hockey season – roughly from the beginning of October to the end of March – 2,000 hockey games are played in the system set up by the Ontario Minor Hockey Association. Every winter, more than half a million Canadian kids play in more than 3,000 rinks. Every year, 1.5 million games are played and 2 million practices are held. In all, at least 2 million Canadians play hockey for fun, while more than 4.5 million are involved in the sport as volunteers, players, or employees.

Given the popularity of the game, it's no wonder that kids from all over Peterborough County tried out for the minor novice Petes. Peterborough and its environs seem to be dedicated to hockey. Even the six ice surfaces within the city are not enough for its 70,000 citizenry, more than 10,000 of whom are involved in hockey – that's one out of every seven people. Within a thirty-kilometre radius of the city, every town, and many villages, also has an arena. These rinks try to accommodate not only boys' and girls' hockey leagues, but oldtimers' leagues for men and women, as well as the OHA Junior Petes and the Tier II Bees. Every winter the sport attracts more than 700,000 spectators, and this number doesn't include those who attend the games of the Peterborough Petes junior team, one of the most successful franchises in junior hockey. In 2000–2001, 521,621 kids played hockey in Canada, and the number of kids playing who were eight and under was growing. In 2000, 71,465 kids played, and in 2001 the number rose to 114,886. Only the older groups saw declines.

Hockey is big in Canada. The Ontario Minor Hockey Association was created in 1940 to benefit youth in the province who wanted to play hockey. It is almost certainly the largest minor hockey organization in the world and concerns itself with players from ages five to twenty. Novice is the biggest age category with more than 20,000 kids between the ages of seven and nine registered every year.

I started coaching in the mites, ages four to six, when my son began playing organized hockey. It was fun. We loved going to the rink. The players changed lines on a buzzer system: as soon as their time was up they had to come off the ice. My son, Scott, was one of the many "scoring stars" and in his second year of mites was moved to the novice level, ages seven to nine. It was still house league, but more competitive. I stayed and coached the mites, but my hockey parent "ego" grew as he played well at the next level.

The next year friends talked us into trying out for the minor novice AAA team, the highest calibre of hockey at that level, a combination of the all-star players in the area. I say "us" because Scott was asked to play and I was asked to help coach. It was a whole new experience. I was an intense person when it came to minor hockey. We were strict coaches. We had fun, but we believed in discipline and playing positional hockey. Winning meant a lot. Not everything, but a lot.

Over the next two years I was an assistant coach and manager of the AAA teams. It was an eye-opener. As an assistant coach you have input, but you're not in charge of the team. As we travelled and played against other teams we witnessed the worst and best in minor coaching. We also witnessed how good the players were and how high the level of play was throughout the province. My expectations for our players certainly changed as I saw the quality of the others.

By the time my son was eleven I thought it would be better if I let others coach him. I was getting too emotionally involved with his successes and failures. I had coached him in lacrosse all summer and hockey all winter for several years. Meanwhile, I helped coach a team of eleven-year-olds in a house league (a lower calibre of play) and thoroughly enjoyed it. It was almost a relief not to have a child on the team.

The next year I helped coach another AAA minor novice team. I knew now that I could get too intense, but even so, I was not as intense as many others.

I managed another team at the bantam level and then dropped out for two years. I was discouraged. It seemed to me that many coaches I'd seen over the years were coaching for all the wrong reasons, and they were not coaching for all the kids. But quitting didn't solve anything. I'd go to the rink and see so many coaches and parents making the same mistakes that I had made: yelling at the players and referees, favouring certain players, ignoring others, taking things far too seriously. So, I went back.

In 1998 I was an assistant with the minor novice AAA team, and the following year with the major novice team. I enjoyed it and picked up many excellent ideas from the people I coached with. After eleven years of coaching mainly AAA novice hockey, I decided I wanted to put even more fun and creativity into kids' hockey. In early 2000, Steve Larmer, a former NHL player who now lives in Peterborough, and I talked about coaching a minor novice AAA team together. We wanted to try to make sure minor hockey was for the children, not for the leagues, the parents, or the coaches. We wanted to see the joy of the game shining on the faces of our players.

Minor hockey coaches are usually volunteers. They should be congratulated for taking the time to coach. In these pages I describe various styles and the methods used by different coaches. Other coaches may disagree with my philosophy, just as I sometimes disagree with aspects of theirs, but I know that we share two key traits: we love working with kids and we love the game of hockey. A number of coaches took the time to talk to me about their coaching styles and methods. I appreciate their generosity in giving me their time and appreciate, too, the dedication and sincerity with which they approach their coaching responsibilities.

There was, and is, ugliness in children's sports. And there was – and still is – lots of evidence things are getting out of hand in arenas across North America. These events all happened within a period of a couple of seasons:

- In Brantford, Ontario, the coach of a team of ten- and eleven-year-old children was charged with threatening to kill a seventeen-year-old referee.
- A man is convicted of beating a youth hockey coach to death in Massachusetts in an argument about practice.
- On-ice officials in Nanaimo, British Columbia, refused to work one weekend because they said they were being subjected to abuse.
- Former NHL star Mark Howe, the son of another star, Gordie Howe, pulled his son out of minor hockey in Michigan because of the pressure. He said, "The bottom line is I never saw Travis [then seventeen years old] smile when he played."
- In Brandon, Manitoba, a summer hockey tournament game for twelve-year-old players ended when a melee erupted. Police were called in.
- A coach of eleven-year-old players in the Metro Toronto Hockey League made his players take off their helmets and get on their hands and knees to push pucks down the ice . . . using their noses, because they weren't passing well enough in the game.
- Mark Recchi of the Philadelphia Flyers told *Reader's Digest* that the biggest problem in minor hockey today is "the pressure parents put on kids. I see it at hockey schools all the time."
- NHL general manager Glen Sather believes creativity by Canadian hockey kids is being lost: "A lot of minor hockey coaches think they're running NHL teams," Sather told the *Globe and Mail*.
- Former Anaheim Ducks' GM, Pierre Gauthier, said, "We need to get more kids on the ice. We need to change the

mentality where you go to an atom game [eleven-year-olds] and the best players are always on the ice and it's all about winning."

• Rick Wolff, in his column in *Sports Illustrated for Kids*, writes: "Unfortunately, too many coaches feel their mandate is to go out and win when every poll shows that 90 percent of kids would prefer to play on a losing team rather than sit on the bench. They just want to play."

—∿∿—

They just want to play the game. That's what Steve and I wanted our kids to do in the season of 2000–2001. Couldn't, and shouldn't, kids have as much fun as the players in old-timers' and beer leagues across Canada? We thought it was possible. This is the story of a year in hockey, a year in which the kids came first.

1

TRYOUTS

"I hate you, Arnold. I owe you for this!" said Steve Larmer, as we looked down at the ice and saw the huge group of kids here for the first hour-and-a-half tryout. There were so many little bodies we could barely see any open ice. Our trainer, John Lawson, was at ice level watching the kids and making sure things ran smoothly.

We had butterflies in our stomachs. We hoped to make the right choices. Imagine, a man who has been through the rigours of NHL stardom, who has won a Rookie of the Year award, a Stanley Cup championship, and an international title – and here he was with butterflies. Then there was me, a forty-eight-year-old editor of a daily newspaper, being nervous about a child's game.

Imagine how the kids, and parents, must feel. Fifty-three kids means roughly a hundred parents looking on, each one believing their little one could be the next Great One, each one dreading the idea that their child could be cut. Some even wondering how they would tell their own relatives and friends that their child didn't make the team. At some level, we were aware of all the conflicting emotions and dreams swirling around the arena – after all, I had been through it myself as a parent. We had to put aside our sympathy for those who would not be chosen and concentrate on the task at hand.

We looked for the kids we thought were the best skaters. We felt if we picked the kids who could skate, we could help them do the rest. And we were picking from the cream of the crop – most of them were the best of their last year's teams. Many of them had played centre, scored goals as easy as spitting, and usually got plenty of ice time on two-line teams. Many of them had skated against weaker skaters and goalies up to this point, but AAA hockey meant they would often be playing against stronger kids. Many parents and kids had no idea how good the competition would be.

Getting the team whittled down would be difficult. After every tryout we spoke to all the kids (with their parents present) – both those who would and those who would not make it to the next round. We talked to the child, not the parent. I wanted to make sure the children knew hockey was *their* game. I'd tell them how hard they had worked and how proud we were of them for trying out. When we were making unfavourable decisions I would say, "Skating is a big part of the game, and if you work on skating everything else will come together. Your balance, shooting, passing all come from proper skating. You even think better if you can skate better. You can go to another team and play as hard as you can, have some fun, and bury that biscuit."

"Does that mean I'm cut?" one vivacious boy had yelled after my little speech. The entire room – Steve, me, our helpers, the kid, and his father – erupted in laughter.

"In other words, cut out the bull," Steve said later. He and I shared the task of talking to the kids who were cut. We both found it a difficult process. If you believe you're making the right decision, you feel comfortable, but never good.

Over the course of the tryouts, some decisions were made for us. One child dropped out with appendicitis; another had to miss the last tryout for a family weekend. By the third tryout, we were down to just over thirty players.

—⚞—

What had brought us here, to make these agonizing decisions? I can sum it up quite easily: our goal as coaches was to give the kids the puck. How we got to that simple philosophy is a bit more complicated.

Both Steve and I believed there were significant problems in minor hockey and we were backed up by the findings at the Open Ice Summit. But it isn't enough to criticize: we felt we had to be part of it to help change it. So we decided to coach an AAA minor novice hockey team. What better place to start than at the youngest level of play? We knew that as the kids got older, fewer and fewer turned out for tryouts. Perhaps it was because the teams become cliques; or because the parents can't find the time to commit to this level of hockey; or because they just don't think it's right for their kids. Or worse, it's possible some kids just don't want to play any more. When a friend of ours coached the minor novice Petes some years ago, he got only seventeen players to the tryouts. In other years when I'd coached we'd usually had between twenty-five and thirty-five. The big turnout this year was unusual – the Steve Larmer factor might have accounted for that.

For several years I had been an assistant coach with the novice Petes – novice is divided into minor, for first-year kids, and major, for second-year kids – and I'd enjoyed those years. I'd already tried out some of my ideas during those years, but, with Steve and Greg Millen's support, I wanted to change things even more. As Steve said, if we were going to "talk the talk, we should walk the walk."

Our philosophy was simple: Let the kids think for themselves. Get rid of the robotic hockey in which the coach controls what the players do on-ice, forcing them to play on their wings or pass the puck as soon as they touch it. We wanted to allow the kids to be creative and develop on their own with the instructors' guidance. In short, we wanted to let kids, and adults, enjoy the game.

We based our team's philosophy on the following thoughts, questions, and ideas we'd been tossing around for years:

—◠◠◠—

Structure. How much do we have to structure children's games? Do we have to structure it at all? Don't they get enough structure at school and at home? Would we yell and scream at kids while they were playing in a sandbox? Do we spend too much time teaching defence to the younger age groups at the expense of offence because it's easier? Hockey, for Steve, "was always sixty minutes of freedom. When I had the puck, I was in control. I was the boss."

Creativity. Do we smother creativity by introducing systems too early? We learn from making mistakes. Have we created a mistake-free environment for our kids to play in? Do we have a no-risk, no-reward system? Should we bench a player for trying to be creative, or reward him or her? If a player turns the puck over at the blue line, does that player miss a shift, or do we encourage him or her to keep trying?

Coaching. Are we coaching for that one kid with special talent who might one day make it to the NHL, or are we coaching for the rest, who never will? Who is responsible for teaching sportsmanship? Shouldn't it be the coaches? Are we too focused on winning? Teaching self-esteem and self-confidence is just as important as teaching a skill.

Parents. The child's and the parents' expectations may be completely different. We felt we needed to educate the parents on the virtues of playing hockey. Hockey teaches life skills, communications, problem-solving, and teamwork. Before the tryouts began, we distributed to all interested parents a leaflet that outlined our approach (see Appendix). Parents who didn't agree with our views could take their child to another team, but at least they would know ahead of time what we were doing.

Business and minor hockey. In minor hockey, each parent pays the same amount of money. It follows that each child should get the same amount of ice time as every other child. When parents stop paying – that is, when the child leaves minor hockey – the amount of time the player plays is at the coach's discretion. Obviously, when players play for teams that pay them – in other words, they are professionals – they have entered a business, and their ice time will be a reflection of their success and skills. When hockey is a business, winning does matter. But in minor hockey, other goals count for more.

—ᘜ—

We don't expect a peewee team to play like an NHL team – it's like teaching a Grade 12 math course to Grade 2 pupils. We were going to allow the players to take chances, make mistakes, and learn from those mistakes. We would also play everyone in all different positions, on power plays, and on short-handed units. They would all get a chance to be on the ice during important points in the game.

The goal was to see improvement in the whole team from September to April. Of course, we know the pursuit of winning is what makes a game fun, but not at all costs. *We would not be a win-at-all-costs team.* We knew some teams in our league would sign fewer players, use fewer players, and shorten the bench (playing only certain players, usually the most talented). We had decided to sign seventeen players because this number would give as many kids as possible a chance to play at this level. We'd win, lose, and improve together.

We decided on the things we wouldn't do: No yelling at referees at any time. No yelling at the kids at any time. Never be negative with the kids. Never shorten the bench. We wouldn't use a game strategy.

And we decided on the things we *would* do. We would allow the kids to understand all the options open to them when they were on the ice. We would let them choose the options, and if that option didn't work, maybe the next time it would. We would ask the parents not to yell directions at the players during the games. Our practices would be as much fun as the games.

Kids – and adults – can develop a passion for hockey. But that passion does not come from winning or losing or even from acquiring particular skills. It comes from being a part of the game, from sharing the exhilaration of the game with teammates, from the sheer joy of skating and shooting and making saves and making plays. If we just let that passion take hold of our young players, everything else will fall into place.

—◊—

Although we wanted the kids to discover the joy of hockey, we were realists. The kids would want to do well, and we would want them to do well. So it was important to pick the players who would be best for the team. These were decisions not to be made lightly. After the fifth tryout, before we made our selections, we consulted the other people we had asked to watch. We reviewed our notes and tossed names and observations back and forth. Only then did Steve and I make our decisions.

Our decisions were not based on the birthdates of the kids trying out, but the issue of age is an interesting one. In 2001, William Hurley, Dan Lior, and Steve Tracze of the Royal Military College of Canada published a paper in which they concluded that "there is a strong relationship between birth month and the chance that a Canadian minor hockey player will play at an elite level. Players born in the early months of the year have an advantage." They took their initial data from the rosters of the Greater Kingston Hockey Association. In minor atom to midget, 87 players were born in the first half of the year; only 18 were born in the second half. When they studied the rest of Canada, they found little difference. Then they studied the National Hockey League. For the year 1996–97, they found 664 players were born in the first half of the year, while 427 were born in the second half. Their verdict was that "the minor hockey system in Canada discriminates against players born late in the year."

I don't know of any coach who looks at birthdates during tryouts. Steve and I looked at nothing except what was on the ice. Did we "age discriminate" without meaning to? Colin Sharpe was a year younger than all the others; he has a January birthday. He made the team because we thought he would be more than able to compete at this level – and we didn't know his age when we picked him. After tryouts I studied the other dates. I found that of the sixteen other players we picked, ten of them were born in the first half of the year, six in the second half. Interestingly, eight were born in the first quarter of the year, and only three were born in the last quarter.

Apart from age, there are other criteria that may sometimes affect selection. A volunteer coach doesn't want to spend his or her winter months with a headache. The first choices are usually obvious but the last ones can be tough. These players may be so close in abilities that trying to pick one over the other is like pulling glass grains from sand. So other factors may come into play. Some coaches make these final picks based on what they know about the players' parents. Some male coaches even base their last picks on the "mother factor." If the mother is good-looking, and all other things are equal, the kid might make the team. I don't know that it really happens very often, but it is a common joke among many boys' minor hockey coaches. We were rather fortunate – we didn't know many of the parents. Our choices boiled down to the kids' talents. So we didn't "parent discriminate." Did we "city discriminate"? In other words, did we favour city kids over rural kids? Amazingly, some parents, especially city parents, worry about this. On our team we had almost an even split 9–8, slightly in favour of city kids.

—\~\~—

At last we had the list of our new team in front of us, and it was time to let the kids in this final batch know who had made it and who had not.

I wanted to do something different when we announced who had made the team. Usually the coach tells the player after the final tryout and away he or she goes. Some coaches phone the players. Others post a list. The minor Petes insist on face-to-face meetings. Today we decided to give the bad news to the last children being released individually and in private with only their parents present. We hoped the parents would realize how young their kids were, that there are so many places to play this wonderful game, and so many years for them to get better. We told them this as we broke the news to them.

Every kid there had hoped to be a Pete, and not being chosen was tough, for us and for them. Some kids cried after they left the dressing room. We were pleased, though, that many parents thanked us for a fair, unbiased tryout. One father jokingly told me later, "At least he can always say he got cut by Steve Larmer." As the disappointed children and their parents left the rink one by one, the tension in the remaining group grew.

Finally, I asked John Lawson, the trainer, to take seventeen kids into a dressing room at the far end of the rink. Steve, Greg (who joined us when we told him his son Charlie had made the team), John, and I met them there. I read out the names of the seventeen players and said, "You are this year's minor novice Petes." We should have had earplugs. The screams were deafening, echoing off the walls of the tiny room. The kids exploded out of the room like they do on the last day of school, screaming.

"I made it. I made it. I made it," shouted Mitch Gillam to his parents, who were waiting in the lobby of the rink. "He had to get right home to tell all his friends to make sure they knew it too," laughs Bill. Then they had to start searching for goalie equipment and the money to pay for it. Another player with equipment on his mind was Kirk Bartley. After shaking hands with his father, Kirk said to him, "Can I get my white

helmet and maroon pants now?" They got them that day. Jeff
Braithwaite was a bit more restrained – he didn't ask for his new
gloves and pants . . . that day.

"The only time I saw any emotion during the tryouts was
when you told him he made the team," says Greg Millen of his
son, Charlie. "That's when I knew that he was really into it. It
was the big smile on his face. He was very excited, but his next
thought was about his buddy who didn't make the team. He was
also very upset for the other little goalie who didn't make the
team." John Hickey says his son, Michael, was ecstatic but also
shocked, adding, "Later, he'd be more shocked when he would
find out how good the team was, how good the players were, and
how good the rest of the league was."

Some kids took it all in stride. "When Curtis made it," says
Cathy Perry, "we just kind of looked at each other. He wasn't
jumping up and down. It was more like 'Okay, can we go home
now?' We weren't first-time hockey parents. Some parents were
crying and kids had tears of happiness, but we've been around
hockey for so long it didn't affect us as much. It wasn't that we
weren't happy. We were."

Paul Donohoe remembers Ryan coming out of the dressing
room, "but not saying much because he was afraid some of the
kids who had been cut might still be around, but once he got out
of the rink he started telling me he had made it." Paul told him
how proud he was of his hard work. Vicki Donohoe was working
at the hospital that day. "I was so nervous," she recalls. Then she
saw Ryan and Paul in the hallway. Ryan was running to her
yelling, "I made it, I made it."

Jordy Coppaway and his daughter, Samantha, were at the
fishing tournament on the last tryout day, so Janice had brought
Wesley. "I was in shock when he made it," she remembers. "I

couldn't find my car in the parking lot." Jordy recalls two cele-brations that day: "We came home with the fishing trophy, and Wesley was all teeth, saying he made it."

Two boys had similar reactions, wanting to share the news with family. "Jeffrey ran right out of the rink," says Darlene Swift. "He had to get right home to call everyone, especially his grandparents and Uncle Jim." "We were shocked at Josh's reac-tion," says Michelle Gregory. "He usually doesn't show any emotion but he came running out of that room, through the doors to the lobby, and yelled to me, 'I made it.' We were so happy for him, but also sad that some of his friends didn't make the team." Colin Sharpe was ecstatic, his father remembers, and when Colin and his mum went for their Sunday supper at Katherine's parents' farm east of Peterborough he told everyone – "grandparents, uncles, aunts, and cousins."

Different families had different ways of celebrating. Dave and Jonathan Nauta went out for a Slurpee. Frank Woodbeck and Stephen went to the driving range to hit some balls. The Bakers took Bradley to the Dairy Queen for a chocolate shake – "A small one," Bradley points out.

Nathan Larson remembered that when his brother Justin made the team, his family had gone for dinner to the restaurant of Justin's choice. The last time Justin had made the team, he had telephoned his mother from the rink and simply said his favourite restaurant's name: "Red Lobster." His mum says, "After Nathan made it, he wanted me to go home so he could phone me and say 'Kelsey's'" [another restaurant].

And then there was the lone girl on the team. "When she made the team she was so excited," says Leslie Gifford, speak-ing of her daughter, Nicole. "She would be playing with all those city select players that she had played against in tournaments."

Neither they, nor Steve and I, knew then how special Nicole's tryout success had been. We had no idea she was the first girl to play for the minor Petes.

—m—

Most Peterborough teams start their practices the week following tryouts, and some communities practise all summer. I decided to give our players the rest of their summer holidays off; they would have enough hockey in the winter. Practices would begin in two weeks.

Steve and I left the rink. The experience had been draining. Why do we have such strong emotions? After all, they're only kids. The answer was simple: it's *because* they are only kids. I had an internal shake, as if the coolness of the rink had somehow moved inside my chest and stomach. Steve also felt the cold. I thought the hot rays of the sun would help soothe me as I stepped outside the arena, but they didn't. My thermostat was stuck.

I put all my equipment, pucks, cones, and training kit into the car and headed for the beer store. As if our two minds were one, Steve pulled his truck in beside mine. We had to chuckle. We were both going home to our swimming pools. After all, it was summer.

2

THE TEAM

Bradley Baker

Dave Baker knew what to expect at Bradley's tryouts. Dave had grown up playing, and trying out, for all-star sports teams. His father, Pat, is in the National Lacrosse Hall of Fame and the Peterborough Sports Hall of Fame. Sheri, Dave's wife, knows her way around an ice rink, too: she had been a figure skater. Bradley's older brother, Tyler, played for the minor novice Petes two years previously, but hadn't gone back. Dave knew he had been labelled as a difficult parent because he had a history of complaining about his son's ice time. He hoped the coaches would see past that and not believe rumours or take it out on his son. He also hoped he had learned from the past.

Bradley started skating at his grandfather Pat's cottage on Chemong Lake when he was two years old. At three he was pushing with one skate and gliding with the other, trying to catch Tyler on the smooth lake ice. "He looked like a scooter out on the lake," Dave recalls with a chuckle. He played his first organized game in Warsaw at four and would sometimes join Tyler's Warsaw team at practices. With his father acting as his coach, he played tykes there for three years, each year getting stronger. During the summer months he played all-star lacrosse, which his dad also coaches. Because Tyler played AAA hockey in Peterborough, the family thought Bradley should get a chance. "At that age, if they are willing to take the challenge, that's fine. He was aware that he might not make the team," says Dave. Sheri adds that Brad wasn't nervous. And echoing so many other parents, she says, "I was more nervous than him."

Kirk Bartley

This was the second time Kirk Bartley had tried out for the minor novice Petes. He had given it a run last year – he'd made it to the last cuts – but the coaches had decided he wasn't ready. This year, the coaches were new.

Mike, Kirk's father, recalls, "The coaches last year took him into the dressing room and told him he had a really good tryout and said next year would be his year." Kirk had put the intervening year to good use. One of his older friends played for the minor Petes and he would go and watch him play. "This year," Mike says, "he knew what to expect. It was a learning experience and he knew what it took to make it."

Mike and Cindy Bartley were both born in Peterborough and are thirty-eight years old. Both have sports in their family backgrounds. Mike played hockey, lacrosse, and golf. In Cindy's family, her dad played some hockey, and her great-uncle was a stellar local hockey goaltender.

Kirk started skating at the age of two. "He'd go watch his sister, Kaley, play hockey and he wanted to play. We couldn't hold him back," says Mike. At age three the coach saw "he could skate and was out of diapers [he was supposed to be four years old to play mite hockey], so he let him play and he did all right."

"I remember his first game," says Cindy, laughing. "They played on half ice and Kirk just kept skating around in circles." They also remember his first goal and have it on video. Mike laughs, too, as he recalls, "I remember he came skating over to the boards to high-five the others and he fell."

Kirk was one of the smaller players at this year's tryouts. When he was in tyke, the coaches would stand him on the players' bench so he could see over the boards. At four, he scored thirteen goals in one game, so he was moved to a higher level where Mike helped coach the team for a year. "I couldn't control my temper on the bench, so I didn't coach again," he says. That is also one reason he watches his son's games from the warm rooms. (These are glassed-in areas above the rink where spectators can watch the games and be close to the snack bar.) When Kirk was five, he was playing with the six- and seven-year-olds and holding his own. In all, he had played organized hockey for five years before this year's tryouts – and he was still only eight.

Cindy found tryouts nerve-racking. The previous year's tryouts had been more tension-provoking than anything they'd experienced so far. This year, not only did Kirk have experience, but so did she.

Kirk woke up that morning asking "When are we leaving?" He knew if he made the team, he'd get a new helmet and pants. He was calm, not nervous, but anxious. At four-foot-three, he was shorter than most of the kids, but with as much spunk as any kid his age.

Jeff Braithwaite

"I don't want to go, I'm not going to make it," Jeff Braithwaite told his parents on the day of the tryouts.

They knew why he was anxious. Jeff had come home from school one day sadly telling his parents that another child had taunted him, "You won't make it, you're the worst defenceman on the ice." His parents also know their blond, almost white-haired, fair-skinned son is a "worrywart."

"I'd quit before I got cut," he told his mother, Karen.

"Winners don't quit, Jeff. Quitters don't win," she told him. Karen and her husband Andy live in Ennismore Township outside of Peterborough. They both attended a local high school where, Andy says, "school got in the way of sports. If it wasn't for sports I probably wouldn't have gone to school." Their children, ages thirteen, eleven, eight, and seven, are all involved in sports. Jeff has been skating since he was three years old, starting on their backyard pond. They call it a pond, but really it's a lighted outdoor rink where the kids spend hours in the winter. Now, at the age of eight, Jeff had already played three years of organized hockey in Ennismore. He was one of the few kids who enjoyed playing defence.

Jeff hadn't said much on the tryout morning, except that he didn't want to make the drive into Peterborough. He's usually quiet and gets quieter when he's nervous. But his parents knew he wasn't content to follow – he "likes to set his bar higher" – so they thought AAA hockey was better for him than a lower level.

Andy and Karen both wanted Jeff to try out for the minor novice Petes. Andy, because he felt Jeff needed a focus, and

Karen, because just going for tryouts would get him more ice time. Besides, they had heard there were a few other kids going in from Ennismore to try out, some of whom had played on Jeff's team last year.

Jeff feared getting cut, but what helped him decide to go was the promise he'd get new gloves and pants. Karen was nervous: "I was afraid of how Jeff would handle it. Andy was far more relaxed. I think hockey and the tryouts are a dad thing." But Andy grew up with friends who played AAA hockey and he says, "I always wanted to play, but wasn't good enough. I always said I'd give my kids the opportunity to play."

Jeff was crying when he got into the family car for the trip to Peterborough. All the way into town he repeated to himself, "Winners don't quit. Quitters don't win."

Wesley Coppaway

"Body contact isn't allowed at this level," we told the big, brown-eyed kid staring at us when we met him in the interview. He just looked down, tugged on the collar of his T-shirt, said, "Okay," then laughed. From the first tryout Wesley Coppaway stood out as a kid who loved to hit, wouldn't give up, and gave it everything he had. At ninety-eight pounds he was the biggest – and most enthusiastic – kid on the ice. But he was bodychecking, and that wasn't allowed in OMHA hockey at the time.

Wesley Coppaway is an Ojibwa who lives in Curve Lake, north of Peterborough. The first known humans in the Peterborough area were the Indian people – the Mississaugas and Five Nations Iroquois lived here at least as early as 1650. In 1818 a treaty was agreed upon between the natives and the Canadian government. The problem was that the Indians who signed it couldn't read, write, or even speak the English it was written in. In an attempt to get the people to farm and convert to Christianity,

the government established the Curve Lake Indian Reserve in
1829. While Christianity took root, farming didn't – the land is
not used much for farming to this day.

The Coppaways have been on the land since anyone there can
remember. Wesley's father, Jordy, was raised there, and his great-
grandfather, also Jordy, was chief for seven years in the 1950s.
Jordy, forty-three and a carpenter, played junior D hockey for
nearby Lakefield more than two decades ago. Prior to that experience, he says, most of his hockey consisted of "chasing the puck
down the lake." Canoe racing and fishing were Jordy's favourite
sports and he remembers dancing in the Curve Lake powwow
at the age of eight. Wesley continues the proud tradition. Jordy's
philosophy for what he wants Wesley to get out of minor hockey
is simple: "He can't dance at the powwow if he's not healthy. He
can't get to school and he can't play hockey without his health.
So I want him to be healthy."

Wesley started skating on the ice of the lake behind their
house. His first organized skating took place in Lakefield, about
a fifteen-minute drive away, when he was five. Janice, his mother,
remembers taking him to the rink. "He wouldn't go on the ice.
It was just skating time. He cried and cried. I had to get my skates
on. He still said 'no way.' I went out on the ice and he came on,
wobbling, hanging on to the boards. I told him to just relax. I
took off down the ice. He didn't even know I could skate and he
killed himself laughing." Laughing is what Wesley does best.

Wesley's never been a goal scorer, but he loves hockey. There
weren't many children his age at Curve Lake so he had to go
to Lakefield to play. In the summer of 2000 he was playing
lacrosse in Peterborough, about a forty-minute drive to the
rink, when his parents saw a schedule for the minor novice
Petes tryouts.

His parents can tell when Wesley gets nervous because "he goes to the bathroom." He went to the bathroom quite a bit on tryout morning. But Jordy and Janice were cool – so cool that they went camping during one tryout, and Janice's mother took Wesley to the rink. Wesley almost dropped out when one of his friends, also trying out for the team, had to quit because he got appendicitis. But his parents told him, "You've come a long way – don't quit now." They wanted him to meet new friends. They reminded him, "When you play with better players, you get better." But the bodychecking would have to go.

Ryan Donohoe

Ryan Donohoe, who has been the top scorer on any team he's played with, learned to skate on a pond when he was three years old. At the time he and his parents, Paul and Vicki, lived in the village of Lakefield, near Peterborough, and Paul would take him by snowmobile to the pond, where Ryan "would deke bulrushes." Paul wasn't above a bit of deception, though; to ensure his son's safety, he made the young lad avoid a hole in the ice by telling him there were "mud monsters" in it. Paul came by his interest in sports honestly: both his parents are athletic. Ryan was constantly playing road hockey and, at the age of five, played his first full year of organized hockey in the local church league. He scored more than 100 goals.

Over the years, Vicki and Paul took note of Ryan's aggressive attitude. "He hates to lose. We've taught him from an early age that if you're going to lose, lose with honour. He's getting better at it," comments Paul. One year Ryan played for two teams in the church league. "We did it to get extra ice time, but about a quarter of the way through the season someone complained, so after that we could play on only one team." The league moved him to a higher age group when he was seven; he was playing against nine-year-olds. At the end of the first game Ryan said to his dad, "Man, those guys are really big," but he kept right on scoring.

Both Ryan and his dad wanted him to try out for the minor Petes. "Part of it was to play against, and with, the best players, the higher calibre, and be more competitive, because Ryan has to be kept challenged." On the morning of the first tryout his whole family – even his younger sister – noticed how quiet he was. Once they were at the rink, though, he was all business. He registered, dressed, and blasted onto the ice. The tryouts were scarcely under way when he went to the players' bench and vomited. Trainer John Lawson and another adult on the ice called Paul over. Paul says, "I took Ryan into the dressing room, calmed him down, gave him a drink of water, took his skates off and told him not to worry, but told him to skate hard. He was dizzy." When he began to feel better, he went back on the ice.

Vicki found tryouts difficult. "I was more nervous for Ryan. He wanted it so much. I wanted it for him." Paul says, "I was concerned that he was sick and not himself. I think he puts pressure on himself. At the second tryout he was back to himself. We had gone back to the cottage the night of the first tryout and went swimming. The next morning at tryouts the difference was like night and day."

Nicole Gifford

She was only four-foot-six and fifty-five pounds, the youngest of four children in her family, but Nicole Gifford wanted to play hockey. Her brother Frank, ten, had played for the minor Petes for the last two years. (This year he tried out for the minor atoms.) Nicole had watched him play and wanted to wear that Petes sweater. The biggest hurdle, and she had no idea it might be one, was that she was a girl and every minor Pete was a boy. In addition, her size might hurt her. Most of the kids were two or three inches taller and twenty to thirty pounds heavier. Nicole's parents, Gene and Leslie, didn't know if their girl had any chance of making the team. They knew she was good and a scrapper, but would she be given a chance?

Gene and Leslie also knew Nicole was different from other girls. She didn't want to play with Barbie dolls. At school, at recess, instead of playing with other girls, she often played soccer or baseball with the boys. In fact, she was so competitive that the other girls at her school wouldn't play with her and she wouldn't play with them.

"As a baby she didn't sleep much through the nights. She was always up," says Leslie. And she was always active. By the time she was three she was skating on the frozen yard in front of their house. "She was the only one of our kids that we didn't have to teach to skate," says Leslie.

By the time she was five, she was playing organized hockey in Ennismore. Nicole had tried out for the minor novice Petes last year at the age of seven. "She wanted to go and when she was cut, she was fine. We told her the chances of making it but she still wanted to try," her parents recall. Now she was getting ready to try again. "She wanted the ice time and she wanted to make the team so she could ride on a coach like her brother," says Gene with a laugh. Gene was nervous about the tryout, but Leslie and Nicole weren't. After all, Nicole had been the top scorer on her male-dominated team the previous year. She was confident.

Some people had phoned the Giffords to tell them that Nicole shouldn't try out for AAA hockey, especially for boys' hockey. Their reasoning? They didn't think sexes should be mixed in the dressing room. "But we ran into Greg Millen, who had coached her before, and he said we should. 'Why not?' he asked."

Nicole jumped in the van on the first day of tryouts. She couldn't wait to get to the rink and get her skates on. She had heard that "Eddy" Arnold was going to be the coach. (I had been an assistant coach on her brother Frank's novice team.) She knew Frank liked me as a coach. Nicole had even heard I might be related to her. "He might be my uncle," she said. (I had married an Ennismore girl who grew up with some of the Gifford clan, but wasn't related to them.)

At the rink, as Nicole performed on the ice, the Giffords could hear whispers about her speed and how well she skated. However, they also heard other comments: "She shouldn't be out there or be in the dressing room with all those boys."

Leslie tried to prepare her daughter for possible rejection. "You might have the ability, but you're a girl," she told Nicole. "It may not be right, but that's the way it is."

Mitch Gillam

The Gillams are a hockey family, although Bill's wife, Carol, didn't grow up in a sports environment. "I'm not a big sports fan but I love to watch our kids play," she says of eight-year-old Mitch and his older brother, Josh, who plays for the peewee minor Petes. When Mitch was three years old, he started skating on the Trent Canal, which freezes every year and is maintained by the city as a long ice rink. If you have skates and live in Peterborough, it's likely you have skated on it at least once. This was where Mitch learned to skate – after a fashion – on the double runner blades that were slapped onto the bottom of his boots. Later he took indoor skating lessons to continue to improve.

Mitch had played four years of organized hockey before trying out for the minor Petes. At ages four, five, and six, he played forward, but his older brother was always taking shots at him in the driveway of their home and he liked it, so in his last year of tyke, he split goaltending duties with another boy. After watching his brother playing for the Petes, he knew he wanted to play for them too, as a forward. His mum, who took him to the first tryout while Bill worked, remembers Mitch sitting in the dressing room beside the two goalies who were trying out. One of the other hopefuls, Stephen Woodbeck, had shouted, "You play net, don't you, Mitch?" One of the tryout goalies, Charlie Millen, looked up at him "with this shocked look on his face." Then Stephen added, "He's got a great glove hand!" Both goalies now looked somewhat concerned. As Carol watched the tryout, she wondered if young Stephen had been right – perhaps Mitch should be there as a goalie, not a forward.

Mitch made it through the first round, but before the start of the second tryout Bill approached me. "Should my kid come out as a forward or a goalie?" he asked. "I notice you only have two goalies trying out and maybe he would have a better chance at making the team." It came out as part question, part statement. I couldn't figure out why he was asking *me*.

"Where is he?" I asked. Bill brought him over. "What do you want to play, forward or goalie?" I asked him. The freckle-faced kid looked at me, flashed a big smile, and with the conviction of an eight-year-old said, "Goalie!"

"Then come out as a goalie," I replied. Bill didn't know what to think. Later he said, "When he went out as a goalie, I couldn't believe I was letting him do this. But sometimes you just have to let them do what they want. I grew up around goalies and I knew the pressure they have. All I said was 'Oh, oh, here we go.'" Because they had to be at the next tryout in six days with goalie equipment, they borrowed from the team Mitch had played for the previous year. And if he did make it, his parents would have to supply his own equipment – the minor Petes do not supply goalie gear.

We were glad to have three goalies trying out – it would make tryouts more competitive. The sad thing was we knew one of the three would be released.

Josh Gregory

Todd Gregory played two seasons for the junior A Petes, from 1985 to 1987. He left the game after he was traded. While he was playing with the Petes, he attended Trent University in Peterborough, but never graduated. He is now a claims specialist living in Bridgenorth with his wife, Michelle, and their four children. "I got sick of the hockey politics. I could have played minor pro but Michelle didn't want to go away and I got sick of hockey," he says. He's quick to add, though, "I got a lot out of hockey – it opens a lot of doors. I met a lot of good friends, but it didn't go the way I expected."

Michelle came to Ennismore from Toronto when she was eight. She played whatever sport was available from baseball to hockey, including all-star girls' hockey in several leagues. In high school she was a star in both hockey and basketball. She and Todd have three sons and a daughter, and Josh is their second-oldest. If Josh made the Petes this year, the Gregorys knew they'd have a busy, and expensive, year. All three boys were playing hockey for different teams.

Josh began to skate near his grandfather's cottage on the frozen Otonabee River, which runs through Peterborough, at the age of three. He started by pushing a chair, a common way to learn balance, but after a half-hour he was skating without it. The next year he was playing organized hockey, then when he was four he got a chance to be goalie in a Thornhill hockey tournament. His older brother, Jake, had been meant to play but backed out at the last minute. Josh, who'd come as a spectator, volunteered to play.

He played four games and excelled, but after that he went back to forward. This was his fourth year of organized hockey.

"He wanted to be a Pete," says Todd. "He saw the pictures of me on our wall and he wanted to wear that Petes uniform. His friends were trying out, and it was all he talked about."

Josh wasn't nervous at all. "After the first tryout, we had to talk to him and tell him that he couldn't just goof around," says Michelle. "It was a nervous time for us," adds Todd. "We didn't think he'd make it," Michelle says. "We know what he has to give, but he wasn't giving it." At the end of the tryouts, they just weren't sure if he'd made it through.

Michael Hickey

John and Lynda Hickey had moved to Ontario from Newfoundland twelve years ago. "When we moved to Peterborough we didn't know how crazy hockey was. When Michael was two years old he would look out our living-room window, see the kids playing hockey on the streets, and he would get a stick and ball to shoot around the house. At first we really didn't want him to play hockey, or get that 'hockey attitude,'" they say. "We wanted him to ski."

Michael had other plans. When he was five years old, he played his first organized hockey on a mites team that played on half ice in a semi-organized spirit. All players took an equal number of two-minute shifts, with each player rotating in goal. But there was a price to pay: The team had 7:00 a.m. practices on Sundays. "Michael didn't get to many of them. He didn't want to go to practice. He wouldn't wake up. When we did take him, he slept while we dressed him and then he'd sleep in the van on the way to the rink. The games were Saturday at 8:00 a.m. And there were struggles. We thought hockey would fade, but as he got better he

got more interested," says Lynda. By the time he was seven
he was bigger than most of the other boys and was scoring three,
five, seven, or even eight goals a game. His coaches started asking
if he would be trying out at a higher level. His parents were
doubtful, but Michael kept after them, so they decided to take
him to hockey school a week before the minor novice tryouts.

They had decided to do this, they say, "Because we saw other
kids were leapfrogging over the others who hadn't been to
schools." As the first day of tryouts loomed closer, they still
weren't sure. They knew he should be playing in a higher calibre
of hockey but didn't know which level was appropriate – house
league, select, A and AA, or AAA.

The first tryout was at 9:00 a.m. That day, Michael had no
trouble waking up. He was nervous, and that meant he was very
quiet. John took him to the rink, while Lynda stayed home with
the three younger children.

"I didn't know what to expect. I certainly didn't think there
would be that many kids. Michael kept asking me, 'Am I good
enough to try out?'" remembers John. He said what most
parents say: "Just try your best." John was more nervous than
Michael – he still wasn't sure about his son trying out. "It's
nerve-racking for parents. I didn't even know the coaches were
in a box watching the players. I thought the guys on the ice
were the coaches until the third tryout. I was always wondering
'Did the coaches see what I saw?'"

Lynda adds, "Hockey is intimidating for parents who haven't
been through the system."

By the third tryout John was convinced they were making the
right decision. "As the tryouts went on I became more nervous
and Michael became less nervous, more confident. But you
could see he was tired. I wondered was it going to be one bad

day and he'd be cut? But I felt confident. If the coaches didn't see what I saw, it would be because they didn't see him at all."

Nathan Larson

Hockey has kept high school teachers Bentley and Annette Larson quite busy. All three of their children play hockey in the winter and soccer in the summer. They live near Buckhorn, on a hobby farm, thirty minutes north of Peterborough and thirty minutes from their teaching jobs in Lindsay. Their lives can get a bit hectic without good time management.

Like many of the parents, Bentley came from a sporting family. He played hockey, volleyball, basketball, and soccer, competed in track, and excelled in rugby. He played in the Ontario Summer Games in 1980 and played five years of rugby at McMaster. He'd also been on the all-Ontario men's team and participated in the national championships in Edmonton. He continued to coach sports while teaching at Lindsay. He has coached all three of his children in minor hockey in Ennismore.

Annette was a sports enthusiast too. She played on volleyball and soccer teams, was a member of a track team, and excelled at basketball, earning the nickname "Elbows." Their oldest boy, Justin, had played for the minor and major novice Petes and was the captain for both. This year he was trying out for the minor atom Petes. Nathan, eight, has been skating since he was four and playing organized hockey for teams in Ennismore. Their six-year-old daughter played for the tyke Ennismore team.

"It takes over your lives. That's the hardest thing. We have no life, but we do it because they love it," says Annette. "We tell the kids to let us know when they don't want to play any more," says Bentley. "Quite frankly we're looking for ways to get out. We can't wait until it's over." But he adds, explaining their sacrifices, "We have them in sports for self-esteem. It breeds success in other areas and gives them a certain reputation with friends and teachers."

Nathan is the opposite of his brother. He's stubborn, moody, and sensitive. But there is one thing he wants to be that his brother is already: a Pete.

"If Nathan didn't make it," said Annette, "my heart would be broken. He would often say, 'I'm just not as good as Justin,' and we'd have to remind him he is two years younger." Bentley was concerned about the possible blow to Nathan's self-esteem: "We were worried about what would happen if he didn't make it and his brother did."

Nathan hides his nervousness by asking questions. On the morning of the first tryout he was relentless. "Will I get cut today?" "Do they call me in after every tryout?" "Where will I play if I don't make it?"

Annette watched the first tryout: "When they were lined up doing races, some of the kids were butting in ahead of him. We talked to him about that after the first tryout and he, innocently, looked at us and said, 'The coaches wouldn't want a cheater on the team.'" "Nathan's strength was team play," says Bentley. "Tryouts are for individuals, so we told him it was like playing hog" [where one player tries to keep the puck from all the others]. They could only hope the coaches saw what they saw.

Charlie Millen

Greg Millen and I have talked for hours about the state of minor hockey in Canada. I had hoped that he would help us coach the team. At first he said he would but his television schedule is a wild one, and he knew he'd miss many games and practices. In the end, however, he changed his mind. He telephoned me from

Dallas. "Don't include me in the coaching staff," he said. His son, Charlie, was trying out for the team as (what else?) a goalie. "I don't want any kid losing a position on the team because I'm the coach. I want Charlie to be on the team because he deserves to be. If he doesn't deserve it, then he shouldn't be on the team." Steve and I agreed. The other goalie trying out was the son of a well-known local goalie who had helped coach in the Petes system. We knew it would be a difficult decision.

Ann Millen, Charlie's mother, says, "We didn't like the idea of having another goalie in the family. The pressure is too much. It sounds selfish, but I kept remembering the times I spent in the washrooms of rinks during Greg's games because fans were yelling and screaming about Greg's play." She adds candidly, "I don't like the sport." Greg nods his head, recognizing her distaste: "She saw the other side of the game as well." He loves the game. Although he hates being on road trips, hockey is his life, and he'd love to coach at the pro level.

Charlie joined organized hockey at the age of four. He played as a forward for two years. He scored quite a few goals in his second year, but then the team started alternating its goalies. He wanted to be one of them. A net had been set up on the big porch of their new Bridgenorth home and soon became a permanent fixture. "He'd play goal and we'd shoot on him. We did that all summer," says Ann. That winter he played goal for the Ennismore tyke select team, where Greg, an assistant coach, was able to see that "he had a lot of natural stuff."

The next summer Greg thought it would be good for Charlie to try out for the minor novice Petes. The Millen household is a busy one. Charlie is the youngest of four; his three older sisters are active, all of them in figure skating. "From the family standpoint I thought if he played for the Petes it would be easier. The team travels on buses so we wouldn't be driving by car to other places. And just to have a schedule of the entire year at the start of the season would get the family more structured." (Many house league teams get exhibition games or practices whenever they can and on short notice.) Although Greg maintains that it was a family decision, Ann says with a laugh that he "didn't consult us totally." She didn't go to any of the tryouts. "One parent there for support was enough. We have three other kids and a cottage," says Ann. Greg tried to keep things low-key for Charlie, but he remembers that he himself was not unaffected: "Tryout time as a parent is very uncomfortable. I wanted him to make the team, but I didn't want people to think he made the team because of my situation." Ann continued to have mixed feelings as the tryouts continued. Charlie was only seven and wouldn't turn eight until December. She knew he'd be one of the younger kids on the team, if he was chosen. Her first concern was for him to have fun, and if he made the team, she knew her second concern would be "How am I going to get him through the winter when Greg's not around?"

Jonathan Nauta

Jonathan Nauta, four-foot-eight and ninety-four pounds, was one of the bigger kids trying out for the Petes. For as long as his parents can remember, Jonathan had wanted to play hockey, and he has, even though he's had little formal skating practice – but he almost quit in mites at the age of five.

"We took him one week, for what we were told was a Can't Skate Program," remembers Dave, "and the coach was doing drills where you had to be able to skate. Jonathan came home and cried and cried that night. We thought he'd never play the game again." But he did go back and he has stuck it out. When

Ed Arnold, Steve Larmer and Greg Millen just before a game in Peterborough.

Wesley "Coppo" Coppoway

Jeffrey "Swifto" Swift

Josh "J.G." Gregory

Curtis "C.P." Perry

Nathan "Trigger" Larson

Riley "Rocket" Rochon

Jeff "Ghost" Braithwaite

Photos by Miranda Studio Photos of Peterborough

THE MINOR NOVICE PETES 2001-2001
FRONT ROW: Riley Rochon, Curtis Perry, Charlie Millen,
Kirk Bartley, Nicole Gifford, Mitch Gillam,
Brad Baker and Colin Sharpe.

Clifford Skarstedt

LEFT TO RIGHT BACK ROW: Jeff Braithwaite, Nathan Larson, Bill Gillam, Jeff Swift, Jonathan Nauta, Greg Millen, Michael Hickey, Ed Arnold, Wesley Coppoway, Stephen Woodbeck, Josh Gregory, Steve Larmer and Ryan Donohoe.

Kirk "Bartman" Bartley

Stephen "Superman" Woodbeck

Michael "Hicksie" Hickey

Ryan "Missile" Donohoe

Bradley "Timbit" Baker

Colin "Wheelsie" Sharpe

Nicole "Jets" Gifford

Photos by Miranda Studio Photos of Peterborough

Mitch "The Thrill" Gillam

Jonathan "Ferrari" Nauta

Charlie "Gloves" Millen

he wasn't at the rinks, he'd go to the "rink" in the basement of their home, a long basement with a net at each end, where he could play with regular or mini sticks. His brother, friends, and father also played there for hours at a time.

Skating gradually became easy for Jonathan, but his biggest advantage was his size – he was usually the biggest kid on the ice. He played for a select team in Ennismore but "wouldn't go out for power skating," so he played for the B team, not the higher-calibre A team, leading it in scoring. Jonathan made the A team the next year when Greg Millen was one of the coaches, and it was Greg who first suggested he try out for the Petes.

"Jonathan wanted to wear that Petes sweater. I think it was an honour thing. Other parents were talking about taking their kids in, and we talked about it. We decided it would depend on who the coaches were going to be. We didn't want a gruff person. We didn't want him to be turned off by a demanding person," says Melody. Jonathan was "a mess" before the tryouts, "a nervous wreck." As soon as he jumped into the pickup truck with his dad for the trip into Peterborough, he started getting queasy. He usually got car sickness anyway, but this was different. Jonathan was quiet in the truck, worried about not performing. His head was bowed and he picked at his fingers as they drove into Peterborough.

Curtis Perry

Greg Perry had applied to coach the minor novice Petes this year. Like all potential coaches, he'd had an interview with the Petes council. He had some coaching experience, having coached the tyke select team the previous winter. This group of excellent players had won forty-six games, lost three, and tied one. Greg, thirty-nine, he felt he knew his hockey.

Greg wasn't taken on as a coach with the minor novice Petes, but he thought he should have been. "What do Arnold and Larmer know about minor hockey?" he asked several people. But he didn't hold a grudge for long – he might not have made the team, but he was still going to take his son Curtis to the tryouts.

Curtis had started skating lessons at three and was one of those kids who took to the business of skating quite naturally. He and his brother Ryan played hockey constantly on the streets or (with mini sticks) in the house. At four years old Curtis was playing mites on the team his dad helped coach. As a forward, he was "always consistent." By tyke he was playing defence regularly. His parents knew Curtis wouldn't put pressure on himself at tryouts – he was a "happy-go-lucky guy, with no high expectations."

"Curtis is more of a playmaker," says Greg frankly. "He passes more and is interested in preventing goals. He gets a little nervous, but not quite as bad as some of the kids. The only thing I told him before tryouts was not to chase the puck, let it come to him, don't run all over the place." Greg and his wife Cathy regarded playing for the Petes as a "natural progression from his four years of previous organized hockey." Although she's not exactly blasé, Cathy recognizes they've gained from their experiences with Ryan. She says, "We've been through it so many times with Ryan, so we're not as nervous as some parents. Ryan was a goalie so it was tougher. Knowing how capable they are helped us, and after the first tryout Curtis was fine. He just wanted to do well." However, they didn't know what to expect if he made the team. "Naturally we wanted him to learn, to play well, at a top level, progress, have fun. Walk out of the rink happy, without pressure. Get better at thinking and skating," says Greg. Cathy agrees. "I wanted him to walk out of the rink smiling. We've seen too many coaches who didn't relate and couldn't be approached."

Riley Rochon

It was a big day for Riley Rochon. His mother was taking him camping for the weekend. He couldn't wait. There was one obstacle. This morning he would have to go to the rink and try out for the minor novice Petes, something he really didn't want to do. But his mother wanted him to do it.

Kathy Rochon is a single mother of two children – besides Riley there's Rachel, twelve – and they live in Peterborough. Kathy is an administrative secretary and a very busy woman. She feared that being involved with hockey would make her even busier but thought it was the right thing for Riley.

Riley had been interested in hockey since he was only three – "He would stand in the backyard and shoot rocks over a six-foot-high fence," Kathy says. "He'd be shooting something all the time, shooting anywhere, on the outdoor rink, in the driveway." Riley had been playing house league for the previous two years against kids two years older than him. Despite that, in one tournament he scored seventeen goals. People started suggesting he play AAA hockey. "He didn't want to, but I thought it would be good for him to try out, so I just took him," she says. "I didn't think that to be always scoring so easily was fun for him or anyone else. He needed to play with people of his talent."

So, in spite of his reluctance, she took him to tryouts. Kathy recalls her own naïveté. "I didn't know we'd have to keep going back for more than one tryout. I was standing beside a mother – I didn't know anyone – and I was telling her about our weekend plans. She told me I had to come back the next morning. Riley wasn't happy about that. I didn't even know you had to pay [fifteen dollars for every hour-and-a-half tryout] for the tryouts."

She couldn't believe how many kids were there and "how good they were." "I didn't think he'd make it. I found it quite stressful. Riley didn't. He wasn't nervous at all. If he made it, that was fine, if he didn't, oh well."

Lloyd Rochon continues to be involved in his son's upbringing. He says Riley has always been independent. "I can remember when he was three, I was trying to teach him how to skate. He wanted to try by himself. I was holding his hand, but he wouldn't let me. He was independent and wanted to succeed by himself." Riley kept falling and getting right back up. "I was reading him a bedtime story that night when I noticed he was all black and blue. He didn't complain. He just slept on his side." Lloyd recalls coming home from work from September to May and finding Riley on the front porch with his hockey stick, a net all set up and waiting to take shots in the driveway with his father. When he was six years old Riley was playing house league, scoring goals regularly. Coaches were telling him to pass the puck, not to score. Asking a kid not to score is like asking him not to lick a melting Popsicle. What the heck's the use? Riley continued to stand in front of the other team's goalie with the puck and wait for the other players to get there. To provide him with more challenge, he was moved to a higher age group and scored a hat trick in his first game.

Lloyd was glad Riley was trying out for the minor Petes and accompanied him to the second round of tryouts. "He's always been confident and knows he can do things. His comment after that second tryout was 'I was third, two others beat me in that one drill.' He didn't like that. I was very proud of him at that tryout. He looked very capable, and I had tremendous pride in him."

Colin Sharpe

Colin Sharpe woke up with a headache on the morning of the first tryout, as did his mother, Katherine. Only seven, he was a year younger than his friends from the previous year's Peterborough selects who were also trying out. The age difference hadn't stopped him from scoring 112 points the previous year, second in team scoring behind Ryan Donohoe.

Katherine had never played team sports, but her brothers had, and her father had coached various teams. In high school she competed in long-distance running but that was about it. Katherine and her husband, Gord, had separated a few years ago but maintained cordial relations. Katherine, a high school teacher, had custody of Colin, but Gord actively shared in the parenting. Gord had played all-star hockey in Cobourg, south of Peterborough. He still holds the record as the leading all-time scorer for the junior C Cobourg Cougars. It enabled him to get a full-deal hockey scholarship at Clarkson University in New York state where he was captain of the Clarkson hockey team. After graduation he got a tryout with the Boston Bruins. He thought he should have made it, but the coach, former NHLer Butch Goring, had a different opinion. Gord played hockey in Britain for a year and a half before he abandoned the dream and returned to the Peterborough area.

Colin was a precocious baby. He started walking when he was eight and a half months old. He seemed to do everything early except go to sleep, usually staying up past 10:30 p.m. He still does this today. Soon after he started walking, he began picking up balls and playing with them. One day he grabbed a hockey stick, looked at his mum, and said, "Mummy, show me how." He started skating at two. Katherine remembers taking him to skating lessons. "I didn't think he'd ever skate. He cried and cried and cried. I didn't want to turn him off it so we quit."

Colin was another of those kids who skated on the frozen Trent Canal. He played his first organized hockey at the age of three and a half, and Gord still remembers his first goal, scored when the teams were using half the ice. "He skated right around both nets and then went to centre ice, just like the Gretzky videos he always watches," says Gord. Colin played underage in hockey and lacrosse and loved to score – he once scored twenty-eight goals in a lacrosse tournament. Gord says, "I told him he couldn't score all the goals and he'd just say, 'Don't worry, I'll pass it.'"

Many of his friends were trying out for the minor Petes. "He was so determined to make that team. There was no wavering," says Katherine, who remembers she had "butterflies that first day, but he was ready to prove himself." She wanted him to make it so he could develop his skills "especially if we were putting in all this time and money." She also felt it would help his self-esteem and would be an introduction to a good hockey system.

Gord noted that Colin had always been a winger and wanted him to have the chance to play other positions. Gord says of the minor novice Petes that Colin was trying out for: "I knew the team philosophy and knew we would enjoy what was coming if he made the team. I just didn't want the team to get pounded; a 50–50 win-loss record would be nice." Katherine says, "Gord and I wanted him to understand there would be a lot of children at tryouts. But he would always say, 'I'm going to be on that team.'"

But the morning of the tryouts, he woke up with a headache. Katherine says, "I hoped he would make the team but I didn't want him to go with a headache. He said, 'Mum, I have to go.'" So they did, and Katherine explained the situation to me. I told them not to worry: "Bring him back the next time." Katherine took Colin home, relieved, but worried that his chances might have been hurt. Colin more than made up for missing the first session in the subsequent tryouts.

Jeffrey Swift

It was a full hour before it was time to leave for the first minor novice Petes tryout. Jeffrey was ready. In fact, he was sitting in his parent's van in the driveway, honking the horn. Such enthusiasm was the norm in the Swift family. Jeffrey's older brother, Mike, who plays for the bantam Petes, would often, at Jeffrey's age, take his hockey stick to bed with him. Hockey is a way of life in the Swift family. Uncles, cousins, friends are all connected to hockey in the winter and lacrosse in the summer. Mike Swift was born in Peterborough. He grew up on a farm in Omemee, just west of Peterborough. His cousin's son, Jeff Braithwaite, was also trying out. Mike had played some hockey in Ennismore and his wife, Darlene, played baseball and hockey. She grew up in Peterborough in a hard-working, sports-enthusiastic family – her brother, Jim, coaches in the minor Petes system.

"Beaver," as they call Jeffrey, started skating on her dad's frozen pond at the age of three. "He'd walk around the house for hours with his skates and guards on – Uncle Jim told him to walk around the house to break them in," says Darlene. Jeffrey took figure skating in Ennismore while he was also playing outdoor hockey. At four he began to play organized hockey. At the time, he could shoot both left and right, but the coaches made him pick one so now he was just shooting left. The previous year, he had played on the Peterborough selects.

The Swifts had mixed emotions about the tryouts. They felt that coaching was the most important thing about kids' hockey. They hated hearing parents talking critically about other kids and boasting about their own. In the end, they encouraged Jeffrey to participate. "Maybe because it was more competitive or because Michael had gone through it," Darlene says. "We thought it would improve his skating, and we knew the skating would be faster. He wanted to go, though. He couldn't wait." She adds, "He gets silent when he thinks about things."

He was silent that first day. He was letting the honking horn do the talking.

Darlene remembers being glad when Jeffrey scored a goal in the first tryout and Mike recalls with a laugh, "Beaver said to us, 'I had a couple of good shots, but my stick was shooting too high.'" But Jeffrey was already looking ahead – as they were leaving the rink, he asked his parents, "If I don't make this team, where can I play?"

Stephen Woodbeck

Julie Woodbeck didn't go to her son Stephen's hockey tryouts. "It was too stressful. I didn't want to see him disappointed," she says.

Frank and Julie Woodbeck live in Mount Pleasant, about twenty minutes west of the Peterborough rink. Frank had played soccer and house league hockey. Julie played house league soccer, field hockey, badminton, and was also a rower. Stephen, a competitive lad, was trying out for the Petes because he wanted to play on a hockey team that "didn't suck." He can be hard on himself, a perfectionist "just like his father." When he'd bring home an 80-per-cent mark on a test, he'd tell his parents sadly, "You're going to be disappointed."

He started playing hockey in the church league when he was four years old, and quickly excelled, scoring 100 goals one year. Bill Gillam was one of his coaches. Stephen was dedicated to the game. It didn't matter where he was, he would play hockey: on the road, on frozen ponds, on outdoor rinks.

So far he'd been more skilled than his teammates, so it wasn't surprising that his parents wondered how well he would compete playing with kids of the same ability. Julie says, "My sister had warned me about tryouts. I'd go over and watch her son and I thought, 'Why are these people getting so worked up? It's just hockey.'" Now, she couldn't deal with the stress of going to her own son's tryouts.

Frank also found tryouts extremely difficult. "It was more stressful than I thought it would be," he admits. "Your child is being judged against other kids. Any parent would be concerned. You wonder what someone else is thinking about your kid. We live and breathe hockey in this city and this country." He adds, "Stephen was stressed, too. He had sleepless nights before the tryouts and got very quiet. One time a friend of his stayed overnight. We were driving the friend home the next day, on our way to a tryout, and the friend kept talking. Finally, Stephen said quite sharply, 'Would you please be quiet.' Stephen didn't say another word for the twenty-mile trip to the rink." And neither did his friend.

3

Getting to Know You

A few kids stood out from the others in tryouts. One in particular was always in the corners chasing the puck like a blackbird swooping down on a single bread crumb. This player showed more speed and aggressiveness than many others. It wasn't the long hair, or that she was the only girl on the ice. It was her pure skating ability. We didn't know Nicole Gifford was seven years old and wouldn't turn eight for another month. We didn't know her selection would bring more attention to the team, a team that had already received attention because Steve and Greg were coaching. But Nicole was the first girl to play for a minor Petes team. A couple of girls had played AA hockey (a lower level of competition, but still all-star) in

Peterborough. One of them, Kalen Ingram, was a super athlete who went on to star for Harvard University and was being touted for Team Canada's women's hockey team. But few girls even tried out for the AAA minor Petes.

"I think it's great," Peterborough Minor Hockey Council vice-president John Currie told *The Peterborough Examiner*. "I saw her in the tryouts and she was an unbelievable skater. I didn't know she was a girl at the time. I don't think it matters if it's a boy or girl. If the kid is good enough to play, you shouldn't discriminate because she's a girl."

Nicole thought it was "neat." "I think it's fun to make the team and it's fun to play with the Petes because it's more challenging. I like that you get to go to new places and meet new people," she said. Her short blond hair, sticking out a few inches below her hockey helmet, bounced as she glided down the ice.

"It's hard to know what this year is going to be like but in other years in the dressing room she's just been one of the guys," her mother said. Leslie and Gene were both concerned that the publicity might make other parents envious and disrupt the team. If any adult was thinking that way they needed to check their heads for marbles. Good publicity for any child is a positive thing. It's something we should all feel good about. I told them not to worry.

As for size, most of these kids are under four-foot-seven and weigh less than eighty pounds. Nicole, even at four-foot-five and fifty-five pounds, wouldn't be the smallest player in our league. In minor novice, bodychecking isn't allowed, so we had no fears about Nicole. The only thing I was worried about was that impish look on her face.

The magnifying glass focused on the team didn't end with Nicole, Greg, and Steve. I had asked John Lawson to be our trainer because he had plenty of experience, was very positive, and loved kids. He had already been a trainer for numerous city teams. Little did I know that before the season started the big Petes would hire him to be an assistant trainer, but after his appointment to the major club, he still decided to stay with us on a part-time basis. Now we had two former NHL stars, the first girl on the minor Petes system, and an assistant trainer with the Peterborough Petes. Some squad!

There was one last late addition. Steve would have some time conflicts with his job at the National Hockey League Players' Association (NHLPA). Greg also had many conflicts because of his CBC job, and now Johnny would be missing many of our games. It was clear I needed another assistant. Bill Gillam wanted the job, and I asked him to join us. He would be dependable, had coached in the minor Petes system, and had volunteered to help. Besides, his son was a goalie. The goalies would be splitting their games evenly throughout the year, making ice time virtually a non-issue for Greg and Bill.

We wanted to use our first practice to test the kids' individual skills. It would give us a benchmark when we tested them again in December and near the end of the season. Many minor hockey coaches don't do this, but how else can you know if your players are improving? Your win-loss record doesn't tell you what is happening with the skill levels of each player.

Holding the first practice on the first day back to school after a long summer was probably not a good idea. I hadn't even thought of this when I had booked the ice. Two kids left the ice with headaches. Check off a learning experience for the coach.

Today was also sweater-number day, always a big day for anyone who plays team sports. You have a certain number, you think it's your lucky number, or the number of your favourite player, or maybe it's a number that one of your parents wore or wears. Kids on this team were no different. Today when I asked them, they screamed the numbers they wanted. When more than one kid wants the same number, we get them to pick a number between 1 and 10; whoever picks the number I have in mind gets their choice of sweater. There was a lot of excitement. Nicole got her favourite number: 10. "That's my brudder's number, too," she yelled and then looked at me with a funny little wink: she squints both eyes, almost closes one of them, then smiles.

Colin Sharpe missed practice with a headache but, although he wasn't there, he got the number he wanted. It was the number his cousin had worn last year, playing for the novice Petes. He was one happy boy when he learned he'd have number 11.

Jeffrey Swift had a special reason for wanting number 16. His cousin, James Johnston, had always worn that number both in lacrosse and while playing for the minor Petes. The number is buried with him. James, a popular city athlete, died at the age of twelve when he was hit by a car as he crossed the road in front of his house. He had been my buddy, and a friend of my son's. I was a pallbearer at his funeral, and it's no exaggeration to say that his death changed my life. It changed many lives. I remember driving to the cemetery in the funeral car. I couldn't believe life outside the car hadn't stopped. Cars were zooming by us. People were busy working, walking, jogging, and talking. Maybe I matured. Maybe I was just getting older. But oddly, children's sports became more fun for me after that day. Sports is not really serious, or consequential, or meaningful. It's not a matter of life and death. Sports is fun.

I hadn't even thought of the meaning of Jeffrey's number request or the fact he was James's cousin. Later, when I saw

Jeffrey skating with the number on the back of his shirt, it came to me. Thank God, he had that number.

—⚹⚹—

We told the kids what we expected of them. No yelling at referees or any other player, no swearing, and no misbehaving on the ice or bench. At the second practice, while some of our friends ran the kids through some drills on the ice, the coaches met upstairs with the parents. We reminded them what we were about and about the philosophy we had given them earlier. I outlined the estimated $12,000 budget for the team and went over the rules (even for parents). I expected some tough questions, but the only question was from one mother who asked, "Will you be helping them with their homework on the buses?" Huh? "No. We're here for the hockey."

There was still one issue: a manager. The manager is an important part of any organized team. He or she looks after the money, keeps the parents up to date on the scheduling, does the finances and other paperwork. I sometimes wonder if parents think all the stuff that happens in a hockey season gets done by magic. I'd already booked the ice time, scheduled the buses and tournaments, created an estimated budget, and got practice jerseys. All these tasks have to be done long before the season begins. We hadn't selected a manager until the season started because we wanted them to be a parent and we didn't want any of the players pre-picked based on their parent being manager.

"We need a manager – any volunteers?" I asked. Lo and behold, someone volunteered. Katherine Sharpe took charge when the meeting ended. (Katherine would hand out so many letters and notices during the year that some of us started calling her "tree killer.") We had another excellent addition to our staff. Some fathers volunteered to help at practice, but we didn't want too many parents involved – we had Greg and Bill and that was probably enough – so we thanked them but declined the offers.

I'd already had some interactions or experiences with parents before the tryouts. On the helpful side, Gord Sharpe had shared with me a list of players and their statistics from the team that he helped coach last year. Less helpfully, another father, whom I had never met, had gone around the city badmouthing me before I was selected. Peterborough is a small community and word gets around. Hockey is emotional, passionate – I knew that. Maybe once this man got to know me, I wouldn't be the "idiot" he thought I was . . . and vice versa.

We would practise every Tuesday and Thursday at 4:30 p.m. Most of our games would be on Saturday and Sunday after-noons. The first practices are always stimulating because you're getting to know the kids and they're getting to know you. I already knew a few kids slightly because I had coached their older brothers previously.

One of those kids was Bradley Baker. I like to give the players nicknames. The previous year I had coached Bradley's brother Tyler and because their last name is Baker, I had labelled Tyler "Doughnut," a name he had taken a liking to. Bradley would usually be in the lobby after our games and practices so I labelled him "Timbit." Timbit was now part of my new team, and he didn't waste any time acknowledging he remembered me. For the first few practices he would sing the following words as he introduced me on the ice: "Ladies and gentlemen, the one and only Eddy Arnold." If pies could smile, that would be Timbit's face.

A day before our first tournament, I had to pick up the team's hockey socks with home and away colours at a local store. The minor Petes system supplies the sweaters and socks; the parents supply everything else. All the players must have maroon gloves and pants and white helmets. Sure, matching colours don't score goals, but the better the kids look, the better they feel.

Running a minor hockey system is not an inexpensive venture. For example, in the previous year the minor Petes council (all volunteer members) spent $96,606 just on ice for games (the teams pay for their own practices). There was $6,500 spent for insurance and $9,672 for referees. The council spent a total of $129,724, but sponsorships, gate receipts, tryout fees, registrations, and other revenues brought in $156,835. The socks are a small part of the council's expenses. (For more details about the dollars and cents of the year described in this book, see Appendix B.)

So here I was picking up the socks and there was a glitch. (It happens more often than not.) The manufacturer had sent the wrong size of white socks. I had to take them, though, because we were in the Pickering Early Bird Tournament the next day. It's a good tournament, not only because it is well-organized, but also because it gives coaches a chance to see their players in game situations before the season starts. We were only into our third week, two weeks before our first league game, and knew it would be interesting and informative. We hadn't put any of the kids in positions yet. Except, of course, for the goalies.

Game day was busy. I had to book an afternoon off work (the first game was at 1:00 on a Friday, a school day, so the kids loved that!) and pick up Steve. I also had to get the team sweaters. Carrying the sweaters is a tiresome chore. I haven't met a coach who likes doing it – I certainly didn't. There are two sets of sweaters – one for home and one for away games. The sets are kept in separate cloth bags. They were heavy and cumbersome but in spite of that I usually forgot them. The sweaters have to be collected from every kid after each game. Coaches discovered the hard way that kids either forget or lose them if it's left to them. But the sooner I got rid of the responsibility for these sweaters – picking them up, taking them home to wash, and bringing them for the next game – and put it in a parent's hands, the happier I would be.

But today our sweaters are in my car trunk along with the socks, pucks, and first-aid kit. Steve is with me as we head to Pickering, about fifty minutes southwest of Peterborough. I would have had the water bottles in the trunk as well if Greg hadn't suggested that the kids bring their own. This would avoid spreading germs and we wouldn't have to carry them around. The kids could keep them in their bags and fill the bottles themselves. A great idea. The less equipment I have to lug around the better.

When we get to the Pickering rink, the Ontario Minor Hockey Association magazine crew was there to interview Steve and Greg. Steve sums up our philosophy in this pithy comment, "There aren't any grizzlies coaching on our bench."

We didn't take buses to tournaments, so the parents had to find their kids rides or also book time off work. It was heartening to see that many of them had made it to this game.

The team and the minor Petes had rules about how the kids were to dress even just to show up for the game. Following these dress rules, Nicole arrived wearing a white shirt, tie, slacks, and dress shoes. "You know, she can wear a turtleneck or blouse," I told her parents.

"She wants to be just like everyone else on the team," her mother replied.

It was nice to see them dressed up, so much better than ball caps, T-shirts hanging out of their jeans, and scuffed running shoes. I could only imagine the trouble they had getting their ties tied, though. Half the parents didn't know how to tie them. ("Do we have to wear ties, too?" Steve had asked. Yes, if you're going to talk the talk . . .)

The dressing room was humming. It hadn't taken the kids long to get used to each other. There were still some quiet ones, but the room was noisy. Picture seventeen players, with all their bags, struggling for space with at least seventeen parents, and three coaches, in a tiny dressing room. We were hanging up the sweaters, stepping over hockey bags, and leaning over parents who were helping their kids dress. Steve never hesitated to help. There he was, the former NHL great, hanging up the minor novice Petes sweaters, and handing out the hockey socks. The same socks I feared would be far too small. Sure enough.

"Hey, these socks are too small!" several kids shouted. Oh well.

We got everyone dressed. I yelled out the positions and lines. The kids had never played together, many had never played the positions I'd just announced, but none of them moaned. I'd taped the captain and assistant-captain letters on some players. You could see in their eyes how proud they were. When they stepped on the ice, they looked in the stands for their parents. I'd decided I was not going to pick a permanent captain or assistants. All the kids would have that chance. Wesley Coppaway was the first captain – he wore a smile wider than a highway; Riley Rochon and Michael Hickey were the assistants.

I reminded the whole team to have respect for the sweaters. "We hang them up after every game. They are our sweaters. They don't touch the floor." Besides, I definitely was not going to pick them all up. There wasn't much to say before the game: "Fill your water bottles, play hard, and let's see what we've put together."

—ω—

The Pickering rink has the players' benches on one side of the ice with the crowd on the other. That's good. One of our rules is that players' parents must stand on the opposite side of the ice from our team. We don't want distractions.

We want the shifts to be about a minute long, but this game starts with three-minute shifts in a ten-minute first period. Steve chews sunflower seeds during the game. "You know, you can change the lines on every twentieth sunflower seed instead of the hundredth," I told him. He laughs and says, "These kids have learned a lot but not how to get off the ice." Greg has a theory about this. (I learned he has a theory about most things.) Because these kids were the best on their teams last year, he figures they had all kinds of ice time and probably only two lines, and aren't used to changing so often.

The game is under way. Greg's son, Charlie, plays well in net against this London team. Steve catches my eye, then yells down the bench so Greg can hear him: "Finally, a Millen who can play net."

The first goal scored against us is a breakaway, a hard shot that beats Charlie on the stick side – he doesn't have a chance – but the game is a tight one. Charlie keeps us in the game. Our team is fast, skates well, and goes after the puck. In the third period we are behind. With only three minutes and sixteen seconds left, our youngest player, Colin Sharpe, ties the game on a shot from in front of the London net that slides by their goalie. Colin lifts his hands in celebration and his linemates converge on him. Our bench jumps with joy. Steve swallows some seeds. Well, maybe not, but he almost chokes when he sees how well we play. Our first game ends in a 1–1 tie. There is only one penalty. It is against us: Wesley Coppaway – two minutes for bodychecking.

—ᴍ—

Steve and Greg were interviewed after the game. ("Don't worry, guys, I've got the sweaters and first-aid kit." Media darlings!) Following the game, I took Steve to lunch in Oshawa, about ten minutes away, at a delightful family restaurant I had discovered when my kids were playing minor sports. After our meal, we went back to the arena for our second game, at 5:30. I was still lugging the sweaters around and looking for Manager Sharpe to find some parents to take them. We were wearing the same colours as in the previous game, so I got the same gripes about the socks.

For this second game, I change all the positions. And again, none of the kids complain. We are playing the home team, Ajax–Pickering. They would be playing in our league this year, so we would see plenty of them in the coming months. Mitch Gillam is in net for this game and he shines. He has to: the opposition is all over us. They score with less than a minute left in the first period; there is no scoring in the second. Kirk Bartley ties the game in the third minute of the final period. The kids are excited. Kirk comes back to the bench with his head bowed, shy about his scoring feat. Five minutes later Ajax scores two goals in less than three minutes. We lose the game 3–1. We lost, but played well. There were only two penalties in this game. One of them was against us, Wesley again, two minutes for bodychecking.

When I picked up Johnny Lawson the next day, he was stocked with red licorice and pistachios. He's just great to be around and the kids love him. Unfortunately, he couldn't make it to many games, but I'll take him whenever I can. Johnny is a former amateur boxer who had varying success in the ring – the shape of his nose suggests he took more than he gave. But giving outside of the ring is something he does freely. If you said one negative word, he had the positive for it. Besides, he actually liked carrying those sweaters around.

We were wearing our white sweaters today. That was good, because I wouldn't have to listen to them whine about how small the white socks were. We handed out the maroon socks.

"Hey, these socks are too big," some of them shouted. It was going to be a long year.

—w—

Today we are playing the Toronto East Enders. Peterborough teams always get more spirited playing against Toronto teams. We love to beat them. It's a chippy contest and we take an early lead. After the first period we are winning 4–1 with goals by Donohoe, Woodbeck, Rochon, and Gregory. Overall, Donohoe gets two goals and two assists while Woodbeck gets another, with singles from Colin Sharpe and Gregory. Gregory gets two assists as well. It is a hard-working team effort. We are winning 7–3 when Steve asks, "If we win this game, do we have to play tomorrow?"

Only if we win this game by eight goals. We all smile. There are four penalties. Toronto takes three and we take one; Wesley, for bodychecking. Three games, three penalties, three body-checks. But the score stays 7–3.

—w—

It was good to hear the kids laughing and enjoying the win, but I had the biggest smile of them all. Some parents had volunteered to look after the sweaters, taking the load from Johnny.

The tournament had shown us the quality of our players – and we were impressed. I wasn't impressed, though, as I walked by a dressing room. A coach was talking, very loudly, to a lone player. He was criticizing the kid for participating in a soccer tournament on the same weekend as the hockey tournament. "You have to commit yourself to this team. You were tired and you let the team down. It's either soccer or us." The coach was shouting. The dressing-room door was wide open for all to see and hear. The kid broke into tears, but the coach continued to berate him.

When I got home I looked at Greg and Steve's winter schedules and wasn't impressed with those, either. Greg was working almost every Saturday night in a Western province doing CBC games. Most Thursday nights he was in Ottawa doing Senators games. We played almost every Saturday and Sunday and practised every Tuesday and Thursday. Someone in the Millen family was going to be busy with Charlie this winter and it wasn't going to be Greg. Steve's job calls for him to be out of town a lot. He would miss about 30 per cent of the games and practices.

—⚬—

At least Greg was available in September. At one of our early practices, he didn't have much luck. He was on the ice when a puck skimmed by his head. He jumped out of the way, fell, and did a flip seals would admire. Later he fell again. I rushed over to see how he was.

"That kid used to trip me last year, too," he said. What kid? There wasn't anyone near him. Steve skated by, rolled his eyes, and mumbled, "Goalies."

This practice was notable for another reason: one of our players broke out of his shell. I knew that as the year progressed, they all would. Wesley is a big, gangly kid, with deep brown eyes that are always smiling at you. In tryouts we had admired his tenacity. He never gave up. If a better skater beat him, he turned and rushed back, doing everything he could to stop the skater.

Another thing about Wesley: he can touch his nose with his tongue. Try it. He does it while he skates. The harder he skates, the closer the tongue gets to the nose.

At this practice we were having a non-contact scrimmage. Wesley nailed two kids along the board. All three went down. He got up quickly, looked at the two still on the ice, and said while skating away, "They're gone!" Wesley was our Eddie Shack, the NHLer who skated like the wind, entertained every time he was on the ice, and had a mind of his own. Wesley blew all over the place. Greg, who would be looking after the goalies and defence (Wesley will probably be a defenceman), considered him "our project." Meaning not *his* project. Steve and I couldn't say enough good things about Wesley. He *was* a hockey player. He just had that attitude of playing the game hard, and having more fun as soon as it was over. I wanted to call him Moose, but thought better of it when I told him and he shouted, "I ain't no Moose!" "How about Coppo?" Coppo he loved. Coppo it was.

If there was an opposite to Coppo on the team, it would have to be Ryan Donohoe. He was one of our fastest skaters. Coppo could look awkward, because he was growing quickly, but Ryan was smooth and slick. He was also quick with his words but far more quiet. During one of our practice skating drills he quit going hard. To encourage him I said, "You could be a leader."

"I am a leader. I'm done," he replied. In other words, the others could follow if they wished.

—◊—

I was in the dressing room before the last practice before our first league game (against Barrie). Timbit had a question. I expected a serious hockey question, or, at least, "What position will I play?" What I got was "Hey, Mr. Arnold, are there movies on the bus? What kind of bus is it?" For most of these kids it

was the first bus trip, their first road game, and it would be the
season's longest. Barrie is almost two hours from Peterborough.
We would take school buses on our shorter trips but for this one
we were renting a coach. Yes, there would be movies.

The cost of the bus was approximately $500. It would leave
our home rink at 11:30 a.m. for a 2:30 p.m. game. It was a long
and expensive trip for a thirty-five-minute game. Too long, and
too expensive, for a bunch of seven- and eight-year-old kids.

—ᴍ—

We have a rule that the team (players and coaches) sit at the front
of the bus, while the parents are at the back. Coppo is sitting
behind Steve and me. As usual, we talk during the trip. Coppo
keeps telling us he can't hear the movie. At one point he tells us,
"I can't hear. Hey, I thought all the adults had to be at the back
of the bus. You guys are adults."

The coach has a washroom, useful when you're travelling with
seventeen little kids. However, this bus has a washroom with a
locked door, as we find out when one kid tries to use it. When
the rest of the bus learns the washroom door is locked, other kids
suddenly have to relieve their bladders. Panic on the highway.
Luckily, the bus driver says there is a skeleton key in his nearby
case. Whew. How do you spell *relief*?

The kids are quiet during the trip. The parents are playing
cards, reading books, marking papers, watching the movie, or
trying to catch a few winks. These kids have frequent-bladder
miles. No sooner do we get to the Barrie rink than more players
have to pee. They shuffle off, their equipment bags over their
shoulders, make their way into the dressing room, only to find
the bathroom door is locked there as well. Their little screams
echo in the dressing room: "I gotta go! I gotta go! I gotta go!"
Coach Gillam has already gone for a key.

There are other problems. Kirk has discovered the team sweater bag doesn't have his sweater in it. Oh, oh. He's in tears. We know he thinks we won't let him play without his sweater. It is getting close to panic time. But there's always a solution. I take one goalie's sweater for him to use and tell the goalie to wear a practice jersey. Then I tape the *C* on Kirk's jersey. His expression changes from tears to smiles in seconds.

We are concerned that there are only two ten-minute periods and a fifteen-minute period. To have such a brief playing time is disappointing. (Peterborough gives three fifteen-minute periods; most of the other rinks give a ten-minute first period, then two fifteen-minute periods.) We're playing all the players as equally as possible and playing them everywhere. Our goalies will play half a game each. That's mainly for the sake of the kids, to get them into every game, but also for the parents, who have travelled a long way. Not to see their child play would be unfair.

It is a great hockey game. Barrie scores the first goal in the first period. Stephen Woodbeck ties it in the second. The play moves back and forth. Little legs are pumping as hard as they can. Steve and I are watching, rather than coaching, the game. The teams trade goals in the third period, with Colin scoring for the Petes. You can hear the parents from both teams cheering on their players, and the coaches from Barrie shouting directions. There are only fifty-one seconds left when Barrie scores to win 3–2. Though it's just the first game of the season, Barrie already has shortened its bench. We see them playing their better players more often than the others. Steve and I have been watching for this, just as we'll watch all the teams. (Oh yes, there are three penalties in the game; Barrie takes two. Ours is for tripping . . . Wesley again. Four games, four penalties. We'll have a talk with him, we say.)

After the game I tell the team, "I'm proud of you guys. You tried so hard." Then Steve goes to each of them, telling them how well they played and slaps their hand (this becomes a tradition). We follow his lead.

Most of the kids are sweating. "What did you do, pour water over your heads?" I ask. They have another question. I expect this will be a good one, considering it's the first league game, the first bus trip, and the first loss of the regular season. Sure enough, it is a dandy: "Hey, Mr. Arnold, are we having pizza on the bus?" Steve and I burst into laughter. Yes, we're having pizza. We plan to do this for the long trips only. The game took only thirty-five minutes to play, but in fact there was plenty of time to play three fifteen-minute periods. The ice is empty after the game, empty well after we've dressed, and still is empty when we leave the rink.

Steve is on his cellphone on the way home making sure his flying lesson is still on when he gets home. He has been learning how to fly a plane for almost a year and is close to getting his pilot's licence. As I sit on the bus and listen to the noise, I wonder if maybe he could buy a plane for the coaches to fly to our games.

He'll be flying to Chicago on a commercial flight this week, missing one practice and our next game, another road trip. Katherine Sharpe has heard that Steve will be away. She's concerned because we're taking the team photos that week. Team photos without Coach Larmer? No need to worry, he'll be there.

Steve is going to Chicago to be inducted into the Chicago Sports Hall of Fame. Chicago fans will always remember Steve. Many restaurants and bars have his sweater or poster on their walls, but it is hard to believe he's the one they so adored as he munches his pizza on the minor novice team bus. He doesn't know it, but I've sent a telegram from our team to Chicago, a surprise message to be read by the master of ceremonies. It reads:

Congratulations on being inducted into the Chicago Hall of Fame. We are very proud of you. We're also very proud that you returned to Peterborough after your excellent hockey career. We know you were once asked why you weren't coaching in the NHL and you replied: "Because Peterborough doesn't have an NHL team." (Hopefully Chicago will have one this year.) We are proud that you were the honorary chairman of Big Brothers/Big Sisters this year in Peterborough. We are proud that you helped start the Pro Hockey Alumni here and helped raise more than $100,000 for children's charity. We are also proud that you chose to give back some of your knowledge of hockey and coach our team this year. We're having fun. Congratulations once again, Coach. Oh, and you missed practice tonight. . . . We'll discuss any disciplinary action when you get back.

When Steve returned home, he said he really appreciated it and added proudly, "I was the only inductee to have a telegram read."

—ᴡᴡ—

Steve is in Chicago. Greg is in Ottawa for another broadcast, a Friday-night special. Bill and I will be on our own for our second league game. We agree to have the bus pick up some parents along the way. The game is in Lindsay, about thirty minutes away, and many parents live along our route. Before we get on the bus, Kirk proudly tells me he was sick and had missed school today. But can he still make it to the game?

"Certainly." Kirk has a cold, but he's feeling much better, he says, as he wolfs down a sandwich.

The bus, a less-expensive school activity bus that the kids and some parents moan about, leaves at 5:15 for a 6:45 game. There are other things I'd like to be doing, but we don't have many of these Friday-night games during the year.

"Hey, coach," yells Riley as the bus pulls away from Peterborough. "We only have one goalie – Charlie's not on the bus."

"You're playing net tonight," I tell him. He looks shocked.

"I don't have any pads."

"We'll stuff some newspapers behind your shin pads."

"Okay."

"Hey, I'll play net," shouts another kid.

"Hey, where's Jonathan?"

"Hey, Wesley's not on the bus – and where's Larse?"

Finally, we have to tell them we're picking up the missing players on the way to the rink. We meet everyone else at a coffee shop about halfway to Lindsay. To my delight Nathan Larson brings some muffins. Last year I coached his brother. His mum makes great muffins, and their little sister started calling me Muffin Man because I ate so many of them. Today one kid sees me eating a muffin.

"Hey, Mr. Arnold, those things make you fart," he shouts. I'm so surprised, I almost spit out the muffin.

"Ooh, you better not fart, coach," another kid says. I can't identify them by voice yet, and they are all behind me. I hardly know their names, let alone their voices. Bill Gillam is laughing. Manager Sharpe doesn't find it very funny. Nicole Gifford is roaring.

About ten minutes later a skunk-like smell enters the bus. "Told you, Mr. Arnold," the kid yells.

We arrive in plenty of time for the game. When we're walking towards the dressing room, a Central Wolves player yells, "We're going to whip you." Timbit gives me a look. I don't know if he heard the kid.

Tonight I change all the positions around again. Kids who have never played forward are playing forward now and those who have never played defence are doing it tonight. I'm sure many parents don't like this, but they know it is our plan. Besides, I think the kids like it.

The Central team doesn't put up much of a fight. They have only one goalie and thirteen players. The coach says that was everyone who came out for spring tryouts. He coaches loudly, yelling at the players, letting them know when they make mistakes. He tells me he just wants the kids to have fun. I believe him, his heart's in the right place.

We win 8–1. Ryan Donohoe, who has more moves than North American Van Lines, gets a hat trick. Colin gets two more goals. Nathan gets one and Nicole scores her first two of the season (you should have seen that smile). Kirk – remember, he was sick all day – gets four assists. Wesley stays out of the penalty box.

As we leave the ice, Timbit skates beside me, looks up at me, and says, "Guess *we* whipped *them*, eh, Mr. Arnold?"

The bus seems to have a few more passengers on the way home. It's packed. Katherine has to sit in the front beside Bill Gillam. Nicole notices this immediately. "Hey, Billie, is that your new girlfriend?" she asks. Amid the laughter, Bill replies, "If it is, you better not tell my wife at the back of the bus."

I look at the smiling Kirk: "Hope you have a cold for the next game, Bartman." His smile broadens and he nods. He likes the nickname and the four points.

Friday is a night my wife and I usually go out for supper. By the time I get home it's 9:30. "Want some supper, honey?" I ask. "Nope, I'm going to bed" is the curt reply. Ahhh, the life of a minor hockey coach!

4

Finding Our Skates

The noise in the dressing room of the Kinsmen arena, our home rink, was louder than in the Evinrude Centre, where our tryouts were held. It could be that the bus trips brought the kids closer and they felt more like a team. Maybe the noise was because all the parents and relatives were there today. Many of those adults were as excited, or more excited, than the kids. Why all the excitement? Today was our first game at home.

It doesn't matter if you're in the National Hockey League or minor novice, the first home game of the season is always special. The fans are there, you want to impress them, and you want to get off to a good start. More important, because it is your home rink, you're supposed to feel better. Minor novice players are no different. The kids, warming up before the game, knew their parents, aunts, uncles, grandparents, brothers, and sisters were in the crowd. Some kids had been offered money to score. Some had been given other types of encouragement to win. Others had been told to try hard. Some of them had been told to have fun.

—⁓—

Pre-game talks are important on any team. We go over the options the kids have and ask them what their options are with the puck in our zone and out of our zone. We tell them the importance of speed on the ice. We say they should be aggressive on the puck.

The kids have started a tradition of handing a puck around to one another in the dressing room. I like them to feel it, toss it, play with it, hold it, and pass it to a teammate. Before every game we will go through the same ritual. I will shout, "Whose puck is it?"

"Our puck!"

"Who are we?"

"The Petes!"

"Whose puck is it?"

"The Petes' puck!"

Greg, Steve, Bill, John, and I are all here for this game. The opposition is Whitby. Many of our kids know about Whitby. They have already played against Whitby teams in lacrosse and soccer all-star games and they know Whitby athletes are tough to beat.

We know the kids are pumped but it doesn't take long to deflate them. Whitby scores two goals in less than four minutes and have a 2–0 lead at the end of the first period. Greg is not impressed by the Whitby coaching staff. He hears them yelling directions at the kids and objecting to referee calls.

"Should I talk to that coach after the game?" he asks me.

"That's up to you, but we should coach our team and let them coach theirs. We're all going to be different during the year," I tell him. Greg accepts this but doesn't accept the yelling.

It is at this game that I get my nickname. The Russian national coach Victor Tikhonov always stood in front of the players' bench while he was coaching. Most coaches stand on top of the bench. In the pros, it's because they are directing the team, they are in charge, and there's nowhere else that commands the attention of the players. I can't understand why this is done in minor novice. I stand in front of the bench because it's easier for me to turn to talk with the players than it is for them to turn, look up, and talk with me. I want them to know we're all part of the same team. Besides, it's more comfortable when you can put your elbows on the boards. I think it looks funny to see grown men standing on top of a bench, their arms folded, their faces forming into scowls as they instruct eight-year-old kids. This night, Mark Vitarelli, one of the minor Petes council members, yells out from behind our bench, "You'd look like Russians if you had the fur hats."

Greg looks at me and instantly labels me "Teak." It stuck for the year.

The Whitby coaches continue to annoy Greg. One coach is yelling, telling kids where to play, when to pass, when to dump the puck, and when to shoot. For our part, we point out the options the player had after he returns to the bench, but we don't tell him he was wrong. The player makes his own decision and tries the play again if he wants to. There is nothing better than watching a kid try the same play a few times, fail, then later succeed with the same play. You can't help being pleased when you see the satisfaction on his face when he returns to the bench.

Referees are the only people paid to be at the game. They try their best, they should know the rules, and they don't need to be verbally abused. When the coaches yell at a referee, it sets a bad example for the players . . . and the fans. I used to yell at referees, too. I would rationalize my actions by arguing that the referee was biased or incompetent. Sometimes I was right, but yelling at him didn't change anything. Referees are human and can behave badly, too. A referee's sarcasm can rile you, but if you take the bait, he has you. I once had a referee give me the finger, right in the middle of a game of eight-year-olds. But most referees know their stuff and do their job well.

Parents are usually the hardest on referees, and today's game is no different. The Whitby fans, who stand beside their own team's bench, aren't taking any lessons from our parents on the other side of the ice. They are screaming at the referee.

"Be fair. Are you blind? Call it both ways? Watch that slashing! They're only kids, let them play!" You can hear this sort of thing in hockey games all over Canada. Sometimes people swear though I don't hear any obscenities today. The situation is so bad in minor hockey that the Canadian Hockey Association has come up with several programs. One is the Shared Respect Initiative that was started in 2000 after the Open Ice Summit, where hockey coaches from all levels got together to discuss minor hockey and make recommendations. Posters and pamphlets were sent to the various leagues for distribution at rinks telling coaches and parents to treat the on-ice officials properly. I still haven't seen even one poster or pamphlet at any of the rinks I've travelled to. Besides, just because the posters are glued on some rink wall doesn't mean people will read them. Tim Renneberg, a journalist and on-ice official, has suggested a better plan: Encourage coaches not to yell, and maybe the parents will take his lead. He would distribute posters to coaches saying, among other things, "My two-year-old has temper tantrums, but forty-year-old hockey coaches shouldn't."

Thirty per cent of on-ice officials in Canada quit the game every year. This high drop-out rate can be partly attributed to verbal abuse. Parents don't seem to care. Tom Clark of the CTV program *W5* described to the Canadian Press, the national news agency, an event that occurred when he was at his nephew's hockey game in Aurora. Parents there knew he was preparing a story on the abuse of referees. "They kidded me about it. Then, for the duration of the game, they heckled and howled at the referee. It was unbelievable." Not so unbelievable, if you've been in minor hockey rinks in the last decade. In fact, it's unusual *not* to hear parents yelling at kids, coaches, and referees. Many leagues have now given referees the power to stop a game, order a person removed from the rink, and not restart the game until that person has left.

Bob Still, the public relations manager for the National Association of Sports Officials in the United States, is disturbed by the trend. He has said, "There is a lack of respect for authority. It's at schools, with the police force, the fire department, teachers, coaches. We see a lack of respect toward authority in society being mirrored in the playing field. You see [professional baseball player] Roberto Alomar spit at an umpire and within two weeks, we had three similar incidents reported. The kids are seeing it happening at the professional level, and it's coming down to them.

"The perspective that parents are bringing into sports is what causes a problem with sportsmanship. Everybody thinks their kid should play at the same level as George Brett. They don't take into account that the kid is learning the game. And, at that level, the official is learning the game too."

Our minor novice games have banned handshakes at the end

of a game. All handshaking must take place at the start of the game. Officials fear a fight or melee will break out while the players are shaking hands.

During the game today our players are all over the place. It's almost like a game of shinny. A good positional team could take advantage of our team at any time, but our kids are never just standing around. They never give up.

We are losing 2–0 at the end of the first period. The Whitby coach brings his players to their bench for a pep talk between periods. Our kids line up for the faceoff. Kirk scores four and a half minutes into the second period. Both teams have plenty of chances but the goalies are playing well. We stage a major come-back in the third period. Colin scores ten minutes into the third to tie the game. Just seven seconds later Jonathan Nauta pops another one.

You can hear the fans in the stands. They are shouting, screaming, yelling encouragement . . . and directions. Whitby pulls its goalie and Jonathan scores again with only one second left. It was a great game for both teams. We know we'll be seeing each other quite a bit this year. We will be playing Whitby, Central, Oshawa, and Clarington at least four times each, and Barrie, Markham, Ajax–Pickering, York Simcoe, and Richmond Hill two games each.

In the dressing room I tell the team how proud I am of them for never giving up. I remind them of the many saves Mitch and Charlie had to make: "Now you know how important goalies are to our team." Coppo, with an answer for everything, yells, "They're not as important as coaches." Smart kid. Today he did a triple spin and came back to the bench to say, "That was a triple Axel." He never stops smiling.

—⁓—

We had had no penalties in the game. At the next practice Coppo told me his father had gone duck hunting. I jokingly suggested to him he'd get more ice time if the coach got a duck.

"Don't worry, I'll shoot you one," he said, smiling. I asked him if he had had a big turkey supper for Thanksgiving.

"No, I had a great supper. I had baloney sandwiches."

Practices are always fun. I had set it up so Steve ran three, then me, then Greg. I wanted to get them both involved and to take advantage of their vast knowledge. Greg was running the first few practices of this month. At the next practice Coppo had forgotten his duck promise. He was walking to his car, spotted me, and asked, "You know what's in our oven, Mr. Arnold?"

"Nope."

"My dad's four ducks," he said.

"What happened to mine?" I asked, feigning surprise.

"You're not getting any," he said and ran away, laughing.

—〰—

Our next game is at home again, against Markham.

Markham hasn't lost a game. I haven't even seen them yet but experience tells me they'll play their best players as often as they can and won't sign too many players. They also pick their team in the spring then play summer hockey. We don't know if our kids or their parents know how successful the other team is. We haven't told them. They'll probably learn today and wonder why.

In most of the teams at this age group, fathers do the coaching. That's good, because they're involved in their children's sports and they are volunteering; it can be bad, though, because they become biased or too strict. However, very few non-parents volunteer their services. It's no different in Markham.

They hit the ice with only twelve skaters and one goalie. Our council feels, and we agree, that the more kids we give the chance to play at this level, the better it will be for more kids. Vito Cramarossa, the coach of the Markham team, has a different philosophy. The nucleus of the team has been playing together non-stop, winter and summer, for twenty-seven straight months. They played a total of thirty-six months straight before a meeting was called at which parents and coaches made a unanimous decision to allow the kids, coaches, and parents to take a break . . . for five weeks the next summer. The members of this team started playing together at the ages of four and five. Vito's philosophy is: "I don't shorten the bench, I'd rather have a shorter bench [to start with] than bring kids that just aren't ready yet." They have 180 practices per year and 92 games. They will participate in 7 tournaments this season. He says he doesn't have any problems with parents: "We've been together a long time, so we're all on the same page." They haven't lost a game in summer, tournament, or league play.

Vito believes in the "work ethic." "If you want to be taught, I'll teach you," he says. "When the kids are at home or school, they can do their thing, but when they're at the rink I want 100 per cent." He believes in "mainly positional play, nothing high-tech." He has been coaching for five years. Before that, he played for the Toronto Marlies junior A team and for the Binghamton Whalers in the semi-pros until he retired in 1989. He also coaches his other son's hockey team of four-year-olds and a soccer team one of his kids played on in the summer. It keeps him busy, but happy.

He credits his team's success to "the team having a winning chemistry and everyone knowing their jobs." He says he changes lines using eight forwards and four defencemen. He rotates players into the centre position during the game. "We started the season with two goalies but one of the goalies decided to play forward and he wasn't good enough here so he moved to A." He also uses power-play and short-handed units.

Markham has some good players. They play their positions well and managed ten breakaways on our goalies – that's right, *ten*. Thank God our goalies are great, so great that Markham scores on only one of these chances. Oh well, we might as well give the goalies some work. We take a 1–0 lead on a backhander by Colin with less than four minutes left in the first period. (The youngest kid on our team is leading us in goal scoring.) Markham ties the game less than two minutes later and the period ends 1–1. Stephen Woodbeck scores early in the second period but Markham gets that one back and another to take a 3–2 lead into the third period.

Markham scores two more goals in the third, but Ryan scores for us too. Ryan hates to lose. Today he slams his stick on the ice in anger when we are scored upon. He also gets two minor penalties.

We lose 5–3, but never quit. Most of our goals are individual efforts whereas Markham goals are scored on positional plays. They are very disciplined and play a structured game, while we are loose and not disciplined when it comes to positional play.

What do you say to the kids after a game like this one? Not much. "We have a game tomorrow. Avoid the girlfriends and –" I look at Nicole "– the boyfriend."

—∞—

The next day, it's another home game. I'm standing outside the dressing room with some parents.

"Anyone have any matches?" asks Greg as he comes out of the dressing room with a pained expression on his face.

"What's going on?" I ask.

"I need some matches, and *don't* go into that room," he grunts. Other parents are also leaving the room quickly. When you enter, you immediately know the reason: "Gas attack!"

"Who let one?" one kid yells. "Hey, it stinks in here," shouts another. Greg finally finds some matches, lights them, then quickly puts them out to let the smell of sulphur drift through the room.

Greg has flown in from Western Canada on the "red-eye," which had to be diverted to Buffalo, because of smog. He doesn't get home until later in the morning – 11:00 a.m. – than expected but he makes it to the rink for a 2:30 p.m. game. He doesn't have to come to the games, but he tries.

Gas emissions aren't the only problem in the dressing room. There is no cash box at the door and nobody from the Petes council to help us. Collecting cash at the door is important because the four-dollar admission charge (parents of home teams don't have to pay) helps pay for referees and ice time. I'm upstairs, after the gas attack, munching on some pre-game french fries; Manager Sharpe will have to look after the money box.

Today's game, against Oshawa, is not much different from the others. I move all the players into different positions again. It's a good game, back and forth with plenty of skating.

"Hey, Eddie," Nicole says during one rush, as she stands beside my right elbow. "My brudder [that's what she calls her brother] plays the next game." Hmm, interesting, Nicole. I tell the kids not to panic with the puck, give them their options of passing, deking, going wide, dumping, and it's up to them to decide the best option for the team. Steve and I give them a word of support every time they come off. It might be "good pass" or "good try" or "nice play, try it again."

We win 3–1. "Hey, Eddie," says Nicole again in the dressing room. "My brudder's playing the next game."

I know what she is telling me so I stay around and watch her brother's game. While I watch, Nicole stands beside me, smiling.

—⟋⟍—

I'm a big Montreal Canadiens fan and didn't hesitate to let our hockey team know about this – frequently.

"How about those Habs?" I'd ask the kids.

"They're no good. They're losers," they'd say. I reply: "Hey, count the Cups. The Leafs haven't won the Cup since 1967. Did they win it on colour television? Or was it on the radio?"

We had only three Habs fans on the team, Josh Gregory (his father was drafted by Montreal), Jeff Braithwaite, and Nicole Gifford. At our next practice a genius arrived at the rink. I saw Colin walking down the hall toward the dressing room, wearing a Montreal Canadiens jacket. I rushed into the dressing room and asked everyone for their attention. Just before Colin entered the room I announced: "I want to introduce the smartest kid on our team, Colin Sharpe." He walked through the door with a smile as wide as a goal crease. Most of the kids started yelling, booing, and cheering for the Leafs. Colin loved it. But it wasn't over yet. He took off his jacket and there, lo and behold, was a Montreal T-shirt. The kid really was a genius. Steve, Greg, Bill, and Johnny were coy – they hadn't said what teams they supported.

Coppo, as usual, had something to say at the end of the day.

"Hey, Mr. Arnold, my dad got a moose." Then, before I could get the words out of my mouth, he laughed and added: "And you're not getting any." He scampered away, with his hockey bag over his shoulder, stick in hand.

We had scheduled the two Barrie games for the beginning of the season so we wouldn't have to drive there during the winter. We wouldn't see this team again unless we faced them in the playoffs in March or April.

The Barrie parents, as did all the other teams' parents, drove their kids to the games in their own vehicles. The Petes council demanded that our kids travel to games on a bus, accompanied by parents. This policy change was made several years ago when a small group of parents and a team official were travelling together to a game. There was an accident. A local volunteer was killed and another person was critically injured. The kids enjoyed the bus trips. The team was together, arrived together, and the parents didn't have to drive. (Some of them did anyway.)

Mike Abram was the Barrie coach. He has coached all three of his sons in hockey. Two of them played at the A level. This year his youngest son was playing AAA. Mike, a high school guidance counsellor who grew up in Midland, played hockey for the University of Toronto and has been coaching high school hockey, for both boys and girls, for fifteen years. He picks the team in the spring, but they don't play in the summer. Mike enjoys coaching the younger kids because "they are like sponges," soaking up the knowledge you give them, he says. His philosophy of coaching is that the amount of ice time players get depends on "who's playing well and who is playing with whom." He knows he has to keep an eye on any parent problems.

At one of their earlier practices he had his first problem. As most coaches do, he puts practice jerseys on his players with specific colours that indicate to the kids with whom they will be playing and on which line. At their first practice, a parent complained that his son "was on the third line" because he was wearing a yellow jersey. He didn't ask the coach about it, he just disagreed and never brought his son back, says Abram. After that one incident, he says, he didn't have parent problems, "or at least not enough for me to say I wouldn't coach again." He admits he "yells a lot" during the games. "It's not anger yelling, it's directional, instructional. I don't wait for practices to do this. You have to do something to get their attention. Whether you call it a passion, I don't know, but I get into it, I'm a yeller."

His team has two practices per week, and two games. About 80 per cent of their practices are held in the early morning – 6:00 a.m. The team gets almost ninety minutes when they practise at that time, compared to the later practices, when they get about fifty minutes. During the practice sessions, he teaches power skating, puck control, and positional play, and introduces different breakouts. He watches the other teams when his team plays them and then sometimes bases a practice on what his team has to do to beat that specific team. He uses a power play, "giving all the kids a chance at the first [games] of the year and later putting the kids who were better in certain situations, especially short-handed units, on the ice.

"Until Christmas we give them all a chance; after Christmas, or in the playoffs or tournaments, we shorten the bench. For the most part we alternate goalies every second game." He finds using the goalies for a full game works well.

What he finds frustrating, he says, is if the kids aren't giving 100 per cent. "We spend a lot of time at the rinks. We're a good hockey team, and I know what we're capable of doing. You get angry because you know what they're capable of doing and it upsets me if they have a stinker.

"I love to coach. I do get into it. I like to see the progression as the year goes on. There's nothing more rewarding when you practise breakouts and then you see it working in a game, the tic-tac-toe for a goal."

—∽—

Today in the game against Barrie I move the kids into different positions. Barrie has control of the game from the start and it's 3–1 after the first period. It's 6–2 after the second. We stage a mini-comeback in the third period to make it 9–5.

Some kids don't like what's happening in this game. "We suck," Stephen Woodbeck complains. Stephen is a very competitive kid. He plays to win, plays hard, is determined, and has a certain biting way with words. "We *really* suck," he repeats later.

It is obvious that we have no idea how to play in our own zone. Several times five kids, all wearing maroon and white, chase the puck. We know the zone play will come but we want to work on skating, shooting, passing, and thinking first. Coach Abram is yelling positions to his players, telling them to stay on their side of the ice, when to pass, shoot, and dump. But Stephen can't get over our play. "Do we ever suck!"

Nine-five is the final score. Five different players score our goals, five players scored theirs. Do we suck? I tell the players after the game to never say we, or anyone else, "sucks."

"You lost this game because *I* suck," I tell them. "I'm putting you guys in all different positions, moving you around, and it doesn't help you win games." I feel badly about losing and their disappointment, but I'm also determined to let them play in all positions.

Coach Larmer, who is out of town, telephones later to see how we did. When I outline the game, he makes an excellent point that puts things in perspective. "I bet you we scored the nicer goals, though," he says.

He's right. On reflection, our goals were creative and showed some individualism. I am grateful, not only for the phone call, but for the way he was able to see the positive.

—⟋⟍—

There were few times the kids didn't want to go to the rink, but one of those times was when our practices featured power skating. Our power-skating coach, who we tried to have come to practices once a month, was Elaine McAuliffe, a former local figure-skating champion.

For these practices, Elaine had full control. The kids were dressed in full equipment and no pucks were allowed. The coaches would go upstairs to watch the kids but that was it – we were there to observe.

Power-skating exercises are good for the kids, but they hated it.

"I can already skate," Colin said.

"This will help you skate better," Steve assured him.

"I can already skate," he said again.

In fact, the kids hated it so much, they tried to figure out when power skating was going to be held and then dress slowly or feign illness. I managed to trick them a few times by changing the schedule, but it wasn't easy. Kirk Bartley took to observing me at every practice. "If you come to the rink with your sweatpants on," his mother told me with a laugh, "he knows it's not power skating. If you're wearing your suit and topcoat he knows it is." I tricked him at one practice by wearing my suit and topcoat and putting my other gear in the coaches' dressing room.

"Oh no, it's power skating," I heard him groan to his mother as I passed the dressing room. His eyes lit up when he saw me on the ice with my gear and the pucks.

"Tricked you, eh, Bartman?" I said, as he skated onto the ice. He took the puck from my stick and skated away, giggling.

Bartman was probably our most intelligent player. He knew where to go on the ice, what to do with the puck, and when to do it. He was also one of the most congenial and hardest-working players. He was usually the first kid at practice. (Steve was usually the first person at practice. He sometimes arrived an hour before a 4:30 practice.)

One day I sang a song to Bartman that he and some of the other kids finished off for me. I sang it to the tune of the *Batman* theme song: "Da-da-da-da, da-da-da-da" and they finished it by shouting "Bartman!"

Kirk liked to be called Batman but I changed it to Bartman. "Batman," he would correct me.

"Okay, Bartman." He'd just shake his head and laugh.

"Hey, Bartman, my mum saw you today," Steve said one day. "And she's going to see you tomorrow. I've told her to watch you, make sure you're behaving." Bartman looked puzzled. "You know that lady that drives your school bus? That's my mum," Steve told him. Bartman was red-faced. Steve and I walked away laughing. Mrs. Larmer has been driving school buses for years. She likes the extra cash, but more than that, she likes the kids. It must run in the blood.

—◊—

"Hey, Mr. Arnold, how come you're always reading news-papers?" asks Wesley as we travel to Whitby on a school night for our 6:30 game. These trips are hectic because the kids have to be on the bus by 4:30 p.m. On the trip they eat some sandwiches or whatever the parents have packed for them. Usually, at least one of their parents can make the trip with us.

"I read so I can learn," I reply to Coppo, who is staring at the page of the *National Post* I have in my hands. (I also have *The Peterborough Examiner*, the Toronto *Globe and Mail*, the *Toronto Sun*, and the *Toronto Star*. We're a five-newspaper hockey team!) "Don't you read?"

"Nope," he smiles.

"How do you learn, then?" I ask. He smiles again and then nonchalantly replies, "I just ask people like you."

"What's new?" I ask Curtis Perry as the bus hums along the highway.

"Nothing," he replies.

"What about *New* York, *New* Jersey, *New* Brunswick?" I ask.

"Or *New*foundland," says Coppo.

Before almost every game I make it a habit to ask one player what he or she learned today. Almost always, the reply has been: "Nothing."

"What a waste of time," I tell them. "Try to learn something new every day. Next time I ask I hope you've learned something." They very seldom do, except for Mitch, who always says he learned "something new in math."

They probably ask five times a trip what time it is and I always give the same answer: "The best time of your life."

"What's that?" I ask Nathan, a quieter member of the team.

"What?" he responds with a smile.

"That," I say again.

"What?" He smiles again. Several members of the team are listening now.

"That stupid look on your face." Nathan shakes his head, laughing with the others, who were roaring.

Later in the dressing room: "Hey, Mr. Arnold, what's that?" asks Coppo.

"I got it at Wal-Mart," I reply.

"What?" he asks.

"That stupid look on your face." The team roars again. All year they tried to catch me out. Politically correct? Who cares – it's team fun.

Bill and I are doing this game alone. Steve is in NHLPA meetings and Greg has flown to Phoenix for a game. For some reason, the bus is the noisiest of the year. One kid has bubble gum stuck on his pants, which then sticks to the bus seat. A mother is trying to get him unstuck. Fortunately, the bus driver is prepared for this eventuality and has some wet napkins. All around us the kids are just jumping.

I find this unexpected level of noise worrisome. "I don't know if this is going to be good, the kids are so hyper," I confide to Bill. Even when we are in the dressing room of the excellent Iroquois Sports Complex in Whitby, the noise doesn't let up. The kids want to know who is going to be captain for this game. They are excited by the announcement. Some groan when they aren't selected, others cheer when they are, and still others pat the new captain on the shoulder, especially the ones who haven't been captain yet. Charlie and Mitch want to know if they'll ever be captains and I have to explain that hockey rules don't allow goalies to be captains or assistants (if they have to ask an official a question, they can't skate all over the ice to get the answer). Timbit is tonight's captain. The look on his face is what makes coaching worthwhile – they all have that look when the letter is taped to their sweater.

The game isn't anything like I thought it would be. Maybe we should always have noisy bus trips. It's the best game we've played. The kids are passing. They're spreading out, skating well. The Whitby coach is yelling, screaming, and really reams out the referee on one penalty call that goes against them.

The coach, Nick Nowak, is a member of the Ontario Provincial Police who grew up in Brantford. He played summer shinny with Wayne Gretzky and Marty McSorley and played hockey in Europe in the 1980s. The previous year he was an assistant coach in minor A hockey; this is his first year as head coach.

He grew up playing all-star hockey and says he's always been competitive. His philosophy: "If you're playing AAA level I'm a firm believer there should be full commitment. It's not winning at all costs, but I demand respect. I make rules and expect them to be followed. We want to have fun, but there are higher expectations in AAA hockey." Many parents and hockey people share this belief. Nick doesn't take summer holidays, so he can take time off in the winter for the five tournaments he has planned for this year's team. The team practises twice a week. Like the Barrie team, the Whitby teams are picked in the spring, but they don't play summer hockey.

Nick is strict with his own rules. He didn't go to parent parties at the end of the year because he knew he would have to cut some of their kids and, as he says, "it's tough because you really get attached to the kids." His practices were "high-tempo, flow drills, skills in a flow system. We do breakouts and defensive work." He also taught passing, skating, and positional play.

Nick's view of our Peterborough team is that it will collapse (a defensive strategy used in hockey): "We found it tough and really had to fight to get through you." Although we never practise or preach any system, the kids just gather in front of our net on their own.

Nick knows he yells during games. "For the most part I let them play. At times I yell encouragement. I had one person helping me who had a kid on the team and he'd be yelling a lot, but he's not coming back. I'm not a hothead, but I would let them know." He says he didn't use a power-play or short-handed unit but has "one, two, or three weaker players who would hurt me when I put them out on a penalty kill or last minute of an important game. So I didn't use them.

"One player missed practices early in the year and never did catch up. I talked to the parents all year and their son didn't get as much ice time. They said they understood, but when I didn't play him as much during the playoffs they told me they weren't happy and probably wouldn't be back. I told them I didn't think he would make it anyway."

In all, the Whitby team has seventeen players. Nick says, "I'm a firm believer that if you have fourteen or fifteen kids you play them all, not like Markham, who would only play ten." The Whitby minor hockey system has an equal-ice-time rule: Each player has to have played the same amount after five games. "But they also understand if you're in a tourney or playoff that it's up to the coach," says Nick. "I picked the team, so I take responsibility. I'm not going to pick the player and then not play them." Parents don't give him many problems, he says, though some have concerns about ice time or their kids "not getting out."

"The important thing is when you don't have a son on the team [Nick didn't], then you're doing what's best for the team. I understand some parents living their dreams through their children. I always confront the parents so there won't be any problems.

"Our defence was a little small when we played teams like Markham and Barrie. Most of the goals were scored against us, in front of our net in scrambles, because our defence couldn't move the bigger players, so we have to get bigger for next year."

—◊—

Our play tonight is outstanding. The kids are skating all over the place. They are the first ones on the puck, win their faceoffs, look for each other . . . and our defence lugs the puck up the ice. (Lugging the puck . . . I remember reading former NHL player Lee Fogolin's comments in an excellent *Globe and Mail* series on minor hockey in Canada: "We wonder why our defencemen aren't mobile and can't handle the puck. Well, go to the rink and watch. The coaches are yelling, 'Get it out! Dump it in! Don't handle the puck!' The kids get the puck and as soon as it's on their stick, it's gone.") Ryan is flyin', scoring two goals. We win the game 4–2.

Just after the game we get the best compliment of our early season. It is nothing about the game on the ice. A Whitby rink employee, a maintenance man, comes over to tell us how much he enjoyed seeing coaches and kids "laughing on the bench."

"You know," he says, "we could use a lot more of that on our kids' benches." We thank him. The next time you're at a minor game, look at the coaches. Why aren't they smiling? Minor hockey isn't serious stuff. If you haven't laughed a few times during a kids' hockey game, you're missing the game.

Our bus ride home is still noisy. Some parents can't believe the noise. Mrs. Coppaway asks how I can stand it.

"Yes, it's tough when kids are being kids," I say with a grin.

"Hey, Mr. Arnold, they're calling me bad names," Stephen Woodbeck complains.

"What are they saying?" I ask.

"They're calling me Woody, Woody Woodpecker."

"Well, Stephen," I tell him, "they must know how tough you are."

"Woodpeckers aren't tough," he responds.

"How come they can peck right through wood, and don't stop until they succeed?"

He smiles, looking satisfied.

—⟋⟋—

At practice, Jonathan Nauta thinks he broke his jaw, or "something below my ear. It hurts when I bite down."

"Want some gum?" I ask. He rests for a minute on the bench then rejoins the action. Sharpie (Colin Sharpe's first, and obvious, nickname) gets hurt going into the boards. Bill looks after him, but lets him lie there until he feels better. A minute later he's still down. I skate to the corner.

"Hey Sharpie, you're not going to be like the rest of the Montreal Canadiens and be injured, are you?" He looks up, gets up, and skates back into practice.

"I guess you can pamper them too much," Bill says with a grin.

I go into the dressing room after the game for a little talk. When I notice Stephen looking at me, I say, "You had a good practice today, Steve."

"Woody, Mr. Arnold, Woody Woodpecker." Okay, Woody.

I remind the team of our next game in Lindsay, the coming Saturday, at what the Central Wolves organization calls Wolves Day.

—⟋⟋—

The Central Ontario Wolves usually play out of Lindsay, but their players come from all over, some travelling an hour to get to practices or games. One day every year they play all the minor Petes teams from minor novice to midget; all the games are at the same rink. It's fun, and the kids love it. Today our team was playing at noon. We didn't take the bus because we thought some parents would want to stay and watch the other games.

The Central organization introduced the minor novices at opening ceremonies and played the national anthem just before our game. It's a big deal for the kids. At five minutes to ice time, Coppo hadn't yet arrived. When he finally walked in, with a big smile, it was just before it was time to go on the ice, but he managed to be ready as we filed onto the ice.

—⁓—

I change all the positions again. Kirk and Josh give us an early 2–0 lead. Riley takes two shots over the net.

"Hey Riley," Steve calls out. "How high's the net?"

"I don't know."

"Four feet high."

Next shift he shoots high again.

"Hey Riley, how high's the net?" Steve asks again.

"I don't know."

"I just told you last time, it's four feet." Steve is laughing. "And where do you shoot the puck?"

"Under the four feet?" That would be nice.

We grin when he returns from a second-period shift after scoring a goal over the goalie's shoulder. Riley has learned how high the net is. He grins back at us.

We have a 3–0 lead going into the third period. Central's coaching staff isn't happy. The coach gives them a talking-to. He throws a towel on the bench to show them how angry he is. (He became embroiled in a major controversy later in the year.) He also starts shortening his bench. He even has kids shadowing some of our players. A very talented player on their team is getting plenty of ice time in the third period, and they mount a great comeback, scoring four goals within six minutes to take a 4–3 lead. We don't quit and get plenty of chances. Woody shoots one over the net with two seconds left in the game. And that is that.

Some kids are down when we enter the dressing room. I remind them the team has to play a full game, not just part of the game. We laugh when I tell Woody he shot a field goal and gets three points for it, just like in football. If they counted the three points, we would have won the game. When I look over at him later, I can see he has watery eyes.

"What's up?"

"My dad's going to yell at me."

"Why?"

"For shooting the field goal."

Funny how kids think. His father doesn't yell at him. Woody had a chance at the end of the game and didn't quit. We make sure we tell him that as long as he has chances, it means he's working hard.

Today is also Nathan's birthday. "I was born in Montreal," he tells me. I didn't know that. "That's why we lost," he says. Smart aleck. (He was born in Peterborough.)

After we speak to the kids some more, Jeff Braithwaite sticks up his hand. This will probably be an important question – he doesn't speak often.

"Hey, Mr. Arnold, can I bring my ghetto blaster for music in the dressing room?" Why not? "Anything but that rap stuff," cautions Coach Larmer.

Finally, I talk quietly with Wesley about his lateness.

"Why were you late?"

"My dad had to get tires."

"You know you're supposed to be here forty-five minutes before game time, don't you?"

He looks at me with surprise all over his face and says, "Not without tires, I'm not."

—ᴡᴡ—

"Hey, Eddie, how come we drive on these buses without bath-rooms?" Nicole Gifford asks, as we head toward an away game with Ajax at 2:30 on a Sunday afternoon. We are travelling in a school bus.

"We just take the big coaches on long bus rides," I answer.

"My brudder's team always takes coach buses," she says. That's good for your brother, Nicole. "My brudder's team has movies on his buses," she adds. Good for your brother, Nicole. "My brudder [he's eleven] takes coaches to all the games, you're just poor!" she announces.

Our bus is a special activity vehicle, a school bus with racks. It's all we needed and was inexpensive. It will cost us $212.93 while a coach would have cost $428.

The team isn't as noisy as on the last trip. The parents must have had a little talk with the kids. Greg, who has been out of town since Tuesday broadcasting NHL games, will meet us in Ajax, about a fifty-minute bus trip from Peterborough. He's coming from Colorado to Toronto and then getting a ride to Ajax from there. He'll ride back with us on the bus. (So you wanted to be a minor hockey coach . . .)

I sit back and enjoy the ride. The scenery is beautiful at this time of year with all the fall tree colours. For a time I tune out the hubbub around me. As usual, the bus is packed. Many parents ride the buses until about peewee, when they either don't enjoy the games any more and are frustrated, or their kids tell them not to come on the buses. By peewee, it's usually only one parent riding the bus.

We arrive in Ajax at 3:35 p.m., Greg shows up about half an hour later. It's so pleasant to see Charlie rushing over to greet him. Those two are closer than spread on a sandwich. The kids are loose while they blast their new-found friend – the ghetto blaster. What had Steve said – "no rap music"? It sounds like rap to me.

"Oh well," says Steve, the philosopher. "It will get the parents out of the dressing room quicker." That it does. The coaches don't linger long either.

The game is going to start late today. No referees have arrived. So our team uses the ice for a practice while the other team stays in its dressing room. Greg runs the practice, in his long black topcoat and his black street shoes. Steve, Bill, and I just sit back and watch him. We can only think of what an exasperated Steve had said about Greg at the first practice: "Goalies!" Steve starts calling him Mike Keenan or Keaner, after the NHL coach who used to do some unorthodox things as coach, including pulling Greg as his goalie several times in a game. Greg starts calling Steve Bob Pulford or Pully, Steve's former general manager in Chicago. Now the three of us have nicknames: Teak, Keaner, and Pully.

When the game finally begins, we're seeing all kinds of good things. The kids are looking for each other for passes. We know positionally they don't look as good as some teams, but they aren't standing around looking and waiting. Following the game, the Ajax–Pickering Hockey Association convener asks if plugging the front of the net with five of our players was our strategy.

"We don't have any strategy, that fools all the teams," Steve replies with a laugh. Our strategy is to be, as Ryan "Missile" Donohoe says, "the fastest team in the universe." He's one of the fastest, thus the nickname. It's more fun to play with the puck than without it, so we tell them to go and get the puck and try to keep it.

Former NHL star George "Red" Sullivan, who played in the Original Six NHL league and was captain of the New York

Rangers, can't believe what he sees in minor hockey today. He told me that when he was a child growing up in Peterborough, the kids didn't have an indoor rink. The parents seldom went to games – "They were working. My mother never even saw me play a game as a pro. When we were kids, we would be on the rink trying to hang on to the puck. You didn't dump the puck in, you wanted to keep it and if you made a mistake you learned from it. I go to the rinks now and the kid's coach yells, 'Stay on your wing.' That's no fun just going up and down the ice. It's too organized. We used to hang on to the puck as long as we could."

The Missile has been launched today. Ryan is flyin'. He scores a hat trick and sets up Josh for another goal. Woody hits the net for our other goal. We win the game 5–1. Ryan is happy only in games we're winning and he's contributing to. He gets frustrated when he doesn't score. Today he's happier than a squirrel in a nut factory.

I tell the kids how well they played and how proud I am of some things they did. Another wise question interrupts our post-game talk. This time it's from Curtis "C. P." Perry.

"Hey, Mr. Arnold, are we getting pizza?" Do these kids ever think hockey?

C. P. gets his nickname from his initials. I have seen those letters every day of my newspaper life for the last thirty years. He has never seen them.

"Hey, how come you call me C. P.?" he asks.

"You're the Canadian Press," I reply.

"The Canadian Express?" he asks. I show him the news-papers where his initials appear at the start of most national stories. He's proud about that. Only momentarily.

"So, are we getting pizzas?" he asks. No. My buses don't stop and we only get pizza on the long bus trips.

"My brudder's bus stops at McDonald's," says Nicole. Good for them. Besides, we're way behind today. The bus is not at the door it dropped us off at, so there is another delay. I know my wife won't be waiting for us to have supper together. She won't be angry, however. She is used to me coaching, the delays and the unusual hours. Usually, a month after the hockey season ends she's asking me to go back to coaching.

Nicole is sitting behind me on the bus trip back. I know this because she keeps hitting me on the head, then ducking, so I can't see her when I look over my shoulder. I look back once, catching her; she has part of a hot dog in her hand.

"Want some, Mr. Arnold?" she asks. Before I can answer, she says "Too bad," and stuffs it in her mouth. Beside her is Mitch, who has lost two front teeth. This has been a process he has shared with me for the last week. He would show me how loose each tooth was by bending it back to his top gum. Not an enjoyable feat to watch, but to him quite an accomplishment. Tonight he's trying to eat an apple. He chews it from the side of his mouth. The next time I look back he has the whole thing stuffed in his mouth.

"My brudder's team would have a coach bus with a movie and a washroom on it," Nicole reminds me again as we make our way down the highway.

The kids have a new game to play on the bus. Every time we are passing a transport truck they yell at the driver. They scream and shout, then repeatedly raise their arms and pull them down, hoping the driver will pull down on his truck whistle. It works sometimes. I just don't understand why they yell. Do they really think that the driver can hear them in his truck?

We can hear them, but we're almost home. We're about a mile from where we park our cars, when a father comes to the front of the bus with his son in hand.

"This kid has to go to the bathroom and it can't wait," Dave Baker says. Timbit is almost in tears. We all understand and ask the driver to stop. We stop at a curve of the road where there is an empty field.

"Listen, we can walk from here," Dave says, as he jumps off the stopped bus with Bradley and heads to some open space. We'll wait. We all know the answer to "How do you spell relief?"

When they come back my big fear is that Timbit will get teased. "Those things happen," I say to the now-smiling, relieved lad. Nobody teases him. It is then I know we have a good team, a team of good kids.

"You know," says Greg. "We just assumed he had to empty the bladder. It could have been much worse."

Other kids start yelling, "I gotta go, too." We tell the bus driver to keep driving. The next time we passed that corner, Jeff Braithwaite yelled out: "Hey, there's Baker's Corners." And from then until year-end, we heard it on every trip we passed it. To this day, when I pass it, I think of it as Baker's Corners.

The Scamp, cute little Nicole, has the final say. She puts her head between the opening of the bus seats and whispers, ever so proudly, in that told-you-so way of hers: "Hey, Eddie, that wouldn't happen on my brudder's bus."

5

NOVEMBER

Pond Hockey

Bill told me one parent wasn't too pleased with the way things were going.

Bill asked him, "What do you mean?"

"Well, I don't call that hockey," was the reply. He didn't like the "pond" type of hockey we'd been playing.

Maybe I'm wrong, but when former professional hockey players tell me they're sick of going to minor hockey games and seeing the kids skate up and down the wing, dump the puck or pass it as soon as they get it, and display no creativity, I think we should listen. When junior and professional coaches say the kids can skate and shoot, but they can't think, by the time they get to those levels, I think we should be concerned. Just what was wrong with the way Canadian kids played hockey forty years ago? Shinny, fooling around, skating, the basics? Isn't that Canadian minor hockey? Pond hockey? That's where George Sullivan, Bob Gainey, Steve Larmer, Wayne Gretzky say they learned the game.

Pond hockey? We had a youth coach years ago who was using Russian breakouts, Montreal systems, walkie-talkies on the bench, and hand signals. He had to be let go halfway through the year.

Pond hockey? It is generally accepted by hockey officials in Canada that the most destructive element in minor hockey is the obsession with winning. A report to the Canadian Hockey Association and Ontario Hockey Federation shows that more than 60 per cent of the coaches distribute playing time based on game situations. In Europe many kids haven't even played games by the age of seven. They are first taught skills, and when they do start playing games their practice-to-game ratio is at least three to one, which is the ratio recommended by the Canadian Hockey Association. The Canadian kids are playing so many games, they don't have time for "pond hockey." They are playing structured, defensive, positional hockey at the age of seven and eight.

Pond hockey? Give me more of it.

Steve is taking over the practices. We had been rotating the duties, with each of us doing three consecutive practices, but it was inconsistent and maybe confusing for the kids. Greg had e-mailed us about the problem after one practice. He didn't think it worked very well: "Teak; Larms – I understand where your heart is in this – keep everyone involved. The problem is when we do this we run the risk of a different focus every three practices without a planned approach."

Okay, I agree. Steve is promoted. When he is asked at one of the alumni hockey games he plays in how the team is going, he says, "Great. I've been promoted to head practice coach." I hope he doesn't want a raise. We joke about this, but in Europe many minor hockey coaches get paid. In Chicago a team of ten-year-olds has a coach from Russia who is paid $35,000 per year. Very few youth coaches in Ontario get paid. The Open Ice Summit has recommended a hockey mentor be hired by organizations to develop and enhance minor hockey programs.

At each practice, we stress skating. For the first time in our two months of existence, we are showing the team some defensive positioning on this day. We'll see what happens in Sunday's game. Steve has a line at one end and Bill has the rest doing some three-on-ohs. Instead of letting them think, Bill's telling them where to pass the puck. I want them to think for themselves, to make up their own minds – I stop the practice and let him know. He agrees. I worry it may take all year to get everyone on the same page.

—◆◆◆—

The kids are ready to play a four-minute hockey game between periods of the Peterborough Petes game. Not surprisingly, both the parents and kids are excited. It's the only Saturday or Sunday we have off until December and a perfect day for grass-cutting, taking leaves from the eavestrough, meeting a few friends, and having a few cold ones. I decide to skip the mini-game.

Our trainer, Johnny, calls to apologize for not being at the last few games. He's going to try to find time to take some licorice to the players at tonight's mini-game. The Petes have been playing most of the same days as us so Johnny feels badly, but the big Petes take priority. We all know that. I'll take Johnny if it's only half the time.

His words have made me feel a bit guilty about not going to tonight's mini-game. I turn to my wife: "Lorna, do you want to go to the Petes game tonight?" It's probably the last place we want to be, but we didn't have anything planned.

The Petes have been around since 1956 and have made it to the Memorial Cup final seven times, more than any other team. They won it once when Gary Green, now a television hockey analyst, was their coach. It's the oldest continuous franchise in the Ontario Hockey League. Every Thursday night about 2,000 people enter the Memorial Centre to watch their Petes, and the team also plays some Saturday night games. This Saturday game has more than 3,000 spectators (probably here to see *our* game, right?), and our kids are pumped.

Most of our team members are dressed in their new Petes jackets, but three or four of them don't have them. The parents make those decisions. If the cost of minor hockey is sky-rocketing, some of the blame has to be laid on these little extras: a jacket ($117), a new Petes hockey bag ($50), several overnight tournaments (they can cost a parent $500 or more a weekend), coaches instead of special activity buses. We haven't asked the parents to get any of the new things such as coats and bags. We're having only one overnight tournament, more for bonding and fun than anything else.

Hockey is only as expensive as one makes it. For example, does all their equipment have to be new? The Canadian government estimates Canadian families spend more than eight billion dollars on sporting goods and services every year. It also estimates that the sports industry employs more than 262,000 people, accounting for more than 2 per cent of the jobs in Canada. None of our kids know about the economic impact or the importance of sports in Canada. Tonight they know only that they will be playing a mini four-minute game against each other between the second and third periods of their local heroes' game.

Coach Larmer is here with his daughter, Bailey. He was helping at a hockey clinic all day at the Memorial Centre. When he got home, Bailey asked if he'd take her to the Petes game. Just what he needed, more hockey. Tomorrow afternoon he's leaving on a deer hunt for a week so he thought he'd better spend some time with her. His wife, Rose, stayed home with a friend.

"I was going to stay home as well, Steve," Lorna assures him; she isn't a hockey enthusiast, but puts up with my love for the game.

The big Petes game is boring. There is no creativity, little hitting, and not much entertainment. You do want something for your ten-dollar ticket. Our kids' game features a hit (I'm sure accidental) of Jonathan on Ryan, and it's a good one. How good? "That's the best hit I've seen all night," says one Petes fan. It may have been the *only* hit all night.

The kids really enjoy their four minutes of fame on the Memorial Centre ice. True to his word, Johnny comes into the dressing room with a big bag of red licorice. Kim Elliott, a local schoolteacher who has come to the mini-game, tells me one of her pupils plays on the team. I ask her to come into the dressing room.

"Bartman, Kirk Bartley, where are you?" I call. He's in the corner of the packed room. "This is Kirk's teacher and she's wondering why he isn't at home doing his school work." Kirk laughs. Kim says hi to a very happy pupil.

"Hey, Mr. Arnold," Wesley says.

"What is it?"

"Come here, Mr. Arnold," he says in a whisper. "Do you have any more licorice?"

There is so much in this bag that most of the players get three pieces each, except Ryan. He doesn't like licorice.

"I'll have his," yell several of his teammates.

Greg and Ann Millen aren't at the game: Greg is in Calgary, Ann is with a daughter at figure skating. Another daughter, Allison, has brought Charlie to the game. She may regret ever getting her driver's licence. It's impressive to see a teenage girl, on a Saturday night, bringing her seven-year-old brother to hockey. She stays, watches, and drives him home again.

The joy of hockey is that it is not a perfect game, Steve comments as we watch the junior game and see the same mistakes our minor novice team makes. I'd rather watch the minor novices' imperfections. Lorna and I leave after the fifty-fifty draw. (No jackpot for the Arnold household.) With ten minutes left in the game, it's 4–0 for London. Enough hockey for tonight . . . except going home and watching Greg on *Hockey Night in Canada*, of course. Tomorrow we're playing a home game.

—⚍—

"Mr. Arnold, I got sick twice today," says a proud Bartman.

"What do you mean, sick?"

"I threw up."

"Why are you at the game?"

"Oh, I'm better now." He smiles and reminds me that the last time he was sick he got four assists. Meanwhile, Ghost's father has called to say Jeff has the flu. (Jeff has been known as Whitey because of his light-blond hair and fair complexion, but I've changed it to Ghost, a name he is very pleased about.) He's "as white as a ghost" and won't be at the game, his father says. I take this opportunity to impress on the kids that if they're sick, they should stay home, because otherwise everyone else might get sick.

It's a home game today against Ajax–Pickering, whom we defeated 5–1 last game. We notice some mothers and sisters are carrying the kids' equipment bags for them. We'll have to stop that. We like to have the kids carry their own equipment. They'll be doing it all their lives, unless they make the pros, so they should get used to looking after their own stuff.

In the dressing room the team passes the puck around. The kids have added a new element to this routine: they bang the puck on their helmets. I talk to them briefly about using their speed, being aggressive on the puck, and using their options. Steve also talks to them about speed, making sure once they pass the puck they keep going so they can get a pass back.

During our warm-up, Greg is getting angry that our players are coming in on the goalies too quickly. One player takes a shot and, in an instant, another player is taking one. To our surprise Greg walks right onto the ice and calls the team together to tell the players to stop it. Steve and I laugh. I've never seen this in minor hockey before . . . that's why we call him Mike Keenan and that's why Steve says again, rolling his eyes, "Goalies."

"Millsy just hates when players shoot like that in practice. He hated it when we played together in the NHL, and that's why I'd always make sure I did it," Steve says with a mischievous grin.

Just before the game, the Ajax–Pickering coaches come over to wish us luck. "Be easy on us this time," they say. That leads me to believe they've been building up for this game. Sure enough, they have a strategy. Because we have Greg and Steve, coaches with a high profile, other teams' coaches make plans and prepare to play us in a way they don't for other teams. They aren't aware that our philosophy doesn't include strategy. Every time we have the puck in their zone, they have a player on their blue line. They know our team will be chasing the puck so chances are, if the puck comes out of the end, the kid on the blue line will be wide open. This is true, but what's that kid on the blue line learning?

Soon the Ajax coach is yelling directions. "Do you think I should have a talk with that coach about kids' hockey?" Greg asks me as the game progresses. That's up to him, but I warn him the other coaches probably won't take kindly to criticism. Later in the game, when the coach starts yelling at the referee, Greg can't hold back any more.

"Take it easy, they're just kids," he calls out.

"You look after your bench, I'll look after mine," is the reply.

Greg thinks minor hockey is losing too many referees because of abuse from fans and coaches. He's right. Across Canada, 10,000 on-ice officials left the game last year, and verbal abuse played a part in those departures. In this instance, the coach does settle down after this little "discussion."

—⚹—

Todd Finlayson was the head coach of the Ajax team and had been coaching for five years. This was his first year at the AAA level. He had a son on the team, as did his assistants. He was coaching because his children played and "with time being what it is, it's nice to be able to enjoy what you're doing with your child." The association arranges one practice per week for the team, and the team found time for one other each week. In Peterborough the association had found us two practices per week.

Coach Finlayson told me that this year, for the first time, the minor novice team was made up of players from the two communities of Ajax and Pickering. Last year they had separate teams. Also, Finlayson had been having some parent problems this year.

"One parent wanted his son to play centre but I told him I was going to play them where I thought they were best suited.

I was going to move the kids all around. Three of the parents didn't like this," he said. The tension became so bad that Finlayson and some of his assistants left coaching when the hockey season was over. They had run into many problems. Some parents wouldn't get their children to the rink thirty minutes before the games as required. A team rule was that if the child was late, he would miss a shift. At one tournament, four kids showed up in the second period. No explanation was offered to the coaches, either during or after the game. The coaches decided to sit the three kids for what he said was a shift in next morning's game. That next morning, when the kids were made to sit out the shift, Finlayson said, some of their parents "started swearing at us during the game. There was a big shouting match in the hallway after the game. We put our heart and soul into the game, then this is what happens."

The parents submitted a letter to the association. The coaches wanted the parents banned from the rinks. In the end, nothing did happen. "We had to put up with them for the rest of the year. We had a fantastic year last year but when the two communities combined their teams, the trouble started. I love coaching kids but I really need to take a year off after this year. It's a real shame."

Despite the problems, he believes some good did come of it. The association hadn't had a code of conduct for coaches and parents in its constitution, but because of this team's problems, one has now been drawn up. They aren't the only association implementing such codes. The hockey association in the small town of St. Mary's, Ontario, has introduced a fair-play code of conduct not only for parents and coaches, but executives and spectators. Programs in the United States and Canada have adopted codes that parents must sign before their child is accepted on the team. The Minor Hockey Association of Calgary, which looks after 12,000 players, introduced a Turning Point Program. The reason for its existence is clearly stated:

> Over the past several years it has become apparent that participating in the game, whether as a player, coach or spectator, has become less and less enjoyable. People are leaving the game for the wrong reason and with bad memories. Conduct of spectators, parents, coaches and players, among and between themselves, is increasingly more unacceptable, both on and off the ice.

Every player, parent, coach, and official has to sign a Fair Play Pledge before they can participate in any of the games. The association president can bar any spectator from the rink for behaviour "unbecoming or detrimental to the game."

Some associations have developed a "rink behaviour policy" with a zero-tolerance commitment. The Windsor Minor Hockey Association is developing what it calls a Fair Play Waiver to be signed by all parents and players. It has a parent conduct code that states, "If any parent/guardian interferes in any manner with an official or player of the [. . .] Association or with the playing of a game, the child of that parent/guardian may be suspended for a minimum of one game, and the matter referred to the board for further action."

One parent, Robert Nutbrown, from Lennoxville, Quebec, has recognized the problems that exist in minor hockey and has taken steps to make hockey fun again. He has formed what he calls an apple-juice hockey league. He says it's like the adults' beer league where you just go to have a good time. In this informal league, the kids learn a few skills but never play in an organized system.

Coach Finlayson, whose day job is as a sales director, says his philosophy is to have a disciplined program. "We expect the kids to listen, to be respectful – and we are as well." He adds, "We teach them more than just hockey." At Christmas, he hooked his team up with the local junior team to tour the Salvation Army specifically to see how the hamper program works during Christmas. They donated about $300 worth of food.

He regards himself as being quiet on the bench. "We would yell encouragement or yell for the player to get on the right side of the ice, but we were never derogatory." He continues, "I've changed my behaviour over the years. When I first started I was quite animated, but I'm a lot quieter now. You grow as a coach no matter what level the team." He didn't shorten his bench very often: "I did more of it when the kids were six, but any time I did it, it didn't work." This year, he did shorten the bench against Barrie, but "I second-guessed myself. I put one of our forwards on defence and sat one of the defence, but Barrie scored and we lost 3–2."

He's had personal experience with what it means to have your child sit out much of a game. His other son had been on an A team and was the "thirteenth or fourteenth player and was always the one who sat when they shortened the bench. As a parent that hurt, but as a coach I understood what the coach was doing."

He believes in teaching his team tactics but rarely used specialty teams – "Maybe only five times and only if the other team was doing it, or in the last two minutes of a game."

—◊—

Today, Coach Finlayson's yelling is getting to Greg. "How can they scream like that?" he asks. I've heard much worse. Greg is new to Canada's minor hockey environment. We're not having a good game today. Most of the play is in our end. This means very long shifts. It also means the goalies are getting another workout. Bill is going to change goalies on the fly without waiting for a whistle, but with Greg's permission. I put a stop to it.

"I don't think we should be hot-dogging [showing off in front of another team]," I tell Greg, who disagrees, thinking it's taking the game too seriously if you can't let the goalies have fun changing while play is going on at the other end of the ice. Could be, but I had talked this issue over with Steve and we agreed changing the goalies on the fly instead of when there is a whistle wasn't the right thing to show the kids. I know the kids love it, so maybe we're wrong.

Mitch and Charlie play well in this game. After the first period we're tied 1–1 with a goal from Nicole. The other team scores in the third to take a 2–1 lead. Greg turns to me after an extra-long shift in our zone and says, "You know what's going to happen on this faceoff? Ryan Donohoe's going to win the draw and take it down to their end and score." The words aren't out of his mouth for five seconds when Ryan does exactly that, scoring a spectacular goal by beating two players and then deking the goalie and shovelling the puck behind him.

"That's why you're on CBC," I say. Then I add, "Now, say it again." He won't and we don't score again. The game ends in a 2–2 tie.

"Missile" is tired. He has speed many kids can only hope for. "Good game, Missile," I say to him. His face shines through the fatigue.

"Mr. Arnold is calling me 'Missile,'" I hear him say to someone.

In the dressing room I get the players to give the goalies a round of applause. The goalies are all smiles. We didn't deserve a tie. Many of our kids were staying on the ice far too long. They do love to play, and every kid wants to get more ice time no matter how hard the coaches try to change the lines. But I saw a lot of good passing, a sign the team is coming together.

Steve has been aching to get to the hunt camp for the deer hunt and he's leaving tomorrow. He hands me the drills for the next two practices scrawled on a piece of paper. In the five years he has hunted (playing in the NHL never gave him this freedom) he has never shot a deer. He's sure he'll get one this time. I remind him to put bullets in the gun. He answers, "I always have bullets. They're in cans, silver bullets." I envy him having that week away. That night, when I get home, I call Ghost. He's feeling better. I tell him about the game, that we tied 2–2, and add that we probably would have won if he'd been there. He laughs and says, "Thanks for callin'."

—⚡—

Coppo is back to his wildlife conversations at the next practice. "Hey, Mr. Arnold," Wesley shouts, "my dad got three deer."

"Hey, maybe he could share," I say.

"We only share ducks," he replies. Short memory, Coppo. He has already cooked and eaten those.

Yesterday Greg was in Atlanta but today he makes it to practice. After that, we won't be seeing him for another week. He's doing three games in the next four days, returning home next Monday.

Mrs. Braithwaite thanks me for calling Ghost after Sunday's game. "He was really excited that you called," she says. That makes my day.

Practice is good. There's a lot of hard work. But Greg has a real problem with one player's attitude. After the kid scored on Charlie, he raised his arms and jumped in victory.

"Geez, that kid's a real hot dog," Greg complains. We both start laughing, remembering he's an eight-year-old "hot dog."

Charlie won't be at practice Thursday or the game Saturday. His sister is in the figure-skating championships in Kingston and he's going with the rest of the family. Many teams wouldn't allow this and would punish the player. Charlie's absence means Mitch will play a full game in goal on Saturday. Charlie will play a full game when he returns Sunday.

The talk at the rink is about a minor atom team in the league that is losing players over the issue of ice time. It seems the father of the star player wasn't happy with the new coach because he was giving kids equal time. Imagine! The complaining must have worked, because the new coach is gone and the old coaches, who favoured playing certain players over others, are back. My own belief is that if the organizations don't support sound minor hockey philosophies, only the great players will benefit. And the great ones will be great, no matter what. They have a passion. They'll play in their driveways, on ponds, in their basements. It's the majority of players, the rest of the kids, we have to make sure keep loving this game. That team will now lose other kids because they aren't playing enough. I'd say goodbye to the star . . . if the parents want him to play elsewhere, let him.

One thing about coaching little kids, you get plenty of colds. The kids are always sniffing, snorting, and running their tongue around their lips to wipe them. Yesterday I woke up with another head cold.

Now, after practice, the parking lot is dark when I leave the rink, lugging my equipment bag along with my stick and bucket of pucks and cones. Little voices can be heard as I walk to my car: "Bye, Mr. Arnold." "See you Thursday, Mr. Arnold." "Hey, Mr. Arnold, we all sweated tonight." "See you, Eddie."

I join in. "Hey, Josh did you pour water over your head to make it look like you were sweating?" Josh lets out a big laugh. The head colds are worth it.

—⚏—

This practice features a new player. He's dropping in for one practice to replace Charlie during his short absence. The kids notice him when they hit the ice.

"Hey, what's that guy doing on our ice?" asks Riley.

"We traded Charlie Millen for him," I reply. Andrew Lytle has come on the ice wearing a sweater for the Lindsay Muskies, a team his father, Mike, helps coach.

"Why does he have that sweater on?" asks Riley.

"What's wrong with it?"

"We're the Petes. That sweater shouldn't be on our ice." Kids learn early. I gather the players at centre ice before the practice and tell them Charlie has been traded.

"Who else did we get?" Riley asks. In spite of the sarcasm, we welcome Andrew by slapping our sticks on the ice.

Wesley's mother is at ice level trying to tell me something. Before she can get the words out, Wesley skates over. "I don't have my jock cup on. I can't find it. My mum lost it."

"Yeah," she says wryly. "As if I wear it."

—⚏—

Today's game is with York Simcoe, which means a long trip to Vaughan, near Toronto. It's a one-and-a-half-hour trip. This time we take a coach. The kids love it and they spend most of the trip quietly watching a movie. Steve is back from the deer hunt. We talk about his lack of success. But he says proudly, "I saw two, though, bounding off." I think he just likes the peace and quiet.

After we unload the gear we learn we're at the wrong rink. Oops. Just as the bus pulls in to the correct rink, it's 11:00 a.m. I ask the kids about the importance of today – they know it is Remembrance Day.

"It's to remember the people who helped fight for us in wars," they say. We have a two-minute silence on the bus.

"Okay guys, let's go out and enjoy our freedom."

Wesley is quiet today, far quieter than usual. Mitch plays great, but we lose 3–0. When a team starts losing, parents usually blame the coach. This is when coaches have to stick to their philosophy. We have a great team and if we wanted to play like robots we might win all our games. Steve stands fast: "We just have to be patient. The team stuff will come." So will the deer, Steve, so will the deer.

The York Simcoe team is good. There is no yelling from their coaches and they are organized. Markham hasn't lost a game this year, but I like York Simcoe's chances of winning the league championship.

After the game, the other team delivers Timbits to our dressing room as a friendly gesture to the visiting team.

"Hey, they're delivering me," shouts Timbit.

A mother from the opposing team wants to talk with Nicole. "I can't believe how good she was, I just want to tell her. She's so cute."

We have pizza on the bus. Wesley is still far too quiet. I suspect something is wrong and sure enough, as we head onto the highway, he vomits. The parents help clean it up while the coaches stay at the front of the bus, pretending to be unaware of what's happening.

Steve and I talk about our team. We are confident we're heading the right way. The kids are getting fair ice time, and they are thinking for themselves. They are also having trouble in their own zone and, while they know where they should be when we ask them, they are all chasing the puck when they hit the ice. We believe that will improve – maybe even at tomorrow's home game, another game Steve and Greg won't be attending. Steve is playing hockey in the NHL Legends of Hockey game in Toronto, and Greg is covering a game in Carolina.

—ɯ—

Johnny is here with Bill and me for today's home game against the Central Wolves. The game is progressing when I hear a loud belch from the region beside my elbow. I look down at the player beside me. Riley has a big smile.

"You have a lot of gas today, Rocket." He just continues smiling.

In the next shift he scores two goals in fewer than twenty seconds. When he finishes his shift, he moves in beside me and without looking at me says, "Yeah, that's a lot of gas, coach."

Riley loves being called Rocket.

"Rocket Rochon, just like Rocket Richard," I tell him.

"Who's he, coach?" Rocket asks.

"One of the best hockey players ever."

"Probably played for Montreal, eh, coach," he says.

Coaching minor novice hockey can be frustrating. You never know what calibre of play to expect and which group of kids is going to show up to play at any given game.

Today, before the game, we had our first chalk talk (and the only one we'd have all year) in the dressing room. We showed them where we'd like them to be in our own zone when our player gets the puck. They seemed to understand. "You are a team. Yesterday you didn't play as a team," I tell the kids before the game, "but the goalie and defence saved your bacon."

"What do you mean, saved your bacon?" asks Timbit. A good question; just what does that mean? The kids start answering it.

"It means you only had cereal this morning," yells one.

"It means your mum didn't cook the bacon," shouts another.

Those answers will do. We win the game 8–2. One highlight for me is when Timbit stops a shot for Charlie. When he comes to the bench, he looks at me with his pie-face smile and says, "Hey, Mr. Arnold, I saved Charlie's bacon, didn't I?"

Another highlight is when the referee comes over and says, "You guys should give the other coaches a clinic." The referee is impressed with our positive way of talking to players and the absence of yelling. He comments on the fact that, after he had blown a quick whistle in the opposing team's end, we hadn't disputed the call. A few minutes later he did the same thing in the other team's zone and the opposing coaches went wild.

Brad Cormier was the head coach of the Wolves, and the adults on his bench were loud. He knew it and made no bones about it. He was caught up in a major controversy with the parents of one of his players. It's not what you like to hear in hockey. The issue had received nationwide publicity – CBC had done a piece about it, as had some Toronto newspapers.

"Life has become a living hell," he said. Brad admitted to kicking a garbage can in the dressing room after a game and acknowledged he yelled at the kids. He denies swearing. After the season was over, he said, "I thought our season would be measured not on wins and losses, but on how hard our team worked. It just ended terrible," and he adds dryly, "Other than that, it was a great year." He says kicking the can was an attention-getter and he knew what he was doing.

Brad, a supervisor for the local water and sewage plant, had been coaching for sixteen years, including coaching a junior C hockey team. "The first thing I preach to the kids is that you get out of it what you put into it. I also tell them if they had to take a penalty, I wasn't going to kill them for that." He said his philosophy was having fun.

Fun is not what Gerry Hickey says his son had with Brad's team. "My boy was scared of him. I got fed up after one game when my boy was crying. I tried to address it with the coach but it didn't happen. Brad was a good practice coach and a good guy away from the arena but he shouldn't be coaching those kids."

The turning point came after one game in November at the York Simcoe rink. The Wolves had lost 7–0. Gerry says, "The coach kept them in the dressing room for forty-five minutes. I've been a coach, trainer, manager, and sponsor, and I know there is more to life than hockey, and the coach should know that." The dressing-room door was shut, while the parents waited outside it for their children. Not everyone agrees that the players were kept in the dressing room for three-quarters of an hour; some say it was fifteen minutes. But Gerry had not been pleased in the past – he had heard the coach call one kid "a puck hog," he had seen his son cry. In addition, a Markham coach, getting ready for the next game, said to some Central parents, "You should be ashamed of yourselves for letting that happen to your children." All in all, it made Gerry feel this was enough.

He went into the dressing room. There, he says, he saw the floor wet with water and strewn with garbage and sticks. At least six boys were crying.

He and his wife decided to pull their son from the team; to do nothing, they believed, would be to tacitly approve of the coach's actions. They sent letters to the Ontario Minor Hockey Association but they claim never to have received a response. They sent letters to the Wolves association, but again they say nothing was done. In 2001 the Hickeys sued the OMHA for not taking action. Then they learned that their son would not be allowed to play minor hockey in Ontario while the suit was pending.

Gerry decided to find out what had happened in the dressing room before he had walked in. He asked members of the Markham team what they had heard. They told him and also agreed to put their stories on paper, in letters to the OMHA. Mark Porter, the Markham assistant coach, wrote:

> While we were going over final preparation [in the next dressing room] with our players for our game we heard a loud crash. What we had heard was the garbage can in the washroom being thrown or kicked over. Immediately after the crashing sound we heard the coach in the adjacent dressing room verbally attack his team. The Central Wolves Minor Novice hockey team had just lost their game and their coach was obviously out of control. This outrage lasted for about 10 minutes.
>
> The tone and the language that was heard was threatening, unprofessional and certainly violated the players' self-esteem. The children were told that they "played like shit" and that "was the worst fuckin' hockey game I've ever seen."

Porter, a schoolteacher, stated, "I have a legal responsibility to report any signs of abuse at my school. As a coach I feel that I have a responsibility to bring attention to this type of behaviour."

Another parent, a doctor, also verified the incident in writing. But the most compelling letter was from Scott Lyall of the Markham team. He wrote, as only a nine-year-old can:

I heard a man screaming out "you guys fucking suck like crap. It's a discrase [sic] that you lost seven to fucking nothing you suck." And then I heard a bang really hard. I thought he through [sic] a child to a door and I was very scared. My coaches heard this and so did my teammates. He was screaming so loud that I could not hear my coach talking.

Brad says he used the word frickin' but admits "even that word is too strong around kids." He says the Markham team wasn't in the room and contends they couldn't possibly know what happened or what was said.

The letters were sent to the OMHA. Brad continued to coach. Gerry, whose son didn't play hockey again that winter, formed the Canadian Hockey Parents' Association to give minor-hockey parents a voice in hockey. He says the only response from the OMHA was that they were leaving the matter in the hands of the Wolves association. In the end, the Hickeys were the only parents to pull their child from the team. Many of the other parents say they still support Brad, and indeed the Wolves appointed him coach of the major novice team for next year.

Steve is back from Toronto for this practice. He was attending the induction of Denis Savard, his friend and former teammate, into the Hockey Hall of Fame. Greg is at practice as well. It is fast-paced and fun. But these fifty-minute practices aren't enough. Every team needs at least ninety minutes. The exercise called British Bulldog ends the practice. Three kids are at centre, the rest are at the end. The ones at the end have to try to stickhandle a puck past the other three.

With Steve running the practices, Greg jokingly (I think) asks what it is that I do. "I delegate . . . or the same as you . . . pick up pucks." Actually, I spend most of the practice asking the kids to listen. Some of them have attention spans about as long as ant hair. I'm really happy with the way Steve is taking over practices. He is into it. After practice I tell the kids, "Make sure you watch the Habs kick Leaf butt on television Saturday night."

—⚏—

Our next game is in Oshawa. We leave Saturday at noon and, unbelievably, Johnny is on our bus. Unbelievably, because he arrived home on the Petes bus early this morning from Kitchener and is coming with us today a few hours later . . . on the same bus he came home on. He loves the kids and the game. I'm especially glad to have him because Steve and Greg are in Calgary.

We get a coach for this forty-five-minute drive today because all the activity buses are being used – and it's not going to cost us any more than our usual bus. The kids watch the movie *Heavyweights*.

"Hey, Mr. Arnold," Missile asks me during the trip, "what's faster – a missile or a rocket?"

I turn to answer him and notice that Rocket is also waiting for the answer. "A missile shoots straight faster than a rocket, but a rocket launches sooner. They are both very quick."

"See, I told you," Missile tells Rocket. Bill Gillam looks over at me, smiles, and shrugs his shoulders.

Our missile is launched very quickly in today's game – Ryan scores just six seconds into the game. There's nothing like a quick goal to pick up a team. The kids are playing well. They're looking for each other and making their own decisions.

Ghost gets his first goal and is all smiles when he returns to the bench. Timbit comes close to scoring his first goal, twice in one shift.

"Darn," he says when he comes back to the bench. "I almost buried the biscuit, Mr. Arnold."

"Right, but the important thing is, you were there. If you keep trying like that it will come."

"A wrist shot over the goalie would have helped," he laughs. These kids are smarter than we think.

In the third period there is a slight disturbance in the area where the Oshawa parents are sitting. A mother is yelling at the referee and anyone else who will listen. She is telling him that our team is too rough. We didn't see that problem. The referees must see it our way because each team gets just two minor penalties in the game.

Charlie makes a big glove save during the game. He has a habit of looking over at me after a big save and I give him the thumbs-up. This time he looks over, removes his catching glove, and gives me a thumbs-up. His new nickname is "Gloves." When the game ends, we win 6–1.

We give Jeff the puck he scored with. "Here you go, Ghost," I say. He's suddenly more concerned about his nickname.

"Hey, Mr. Arnold, what happened to Whitey?" he asks.

"Who's Whitey?"

"That's what you used to call me before Ghost."

"Oh, which do you like better?"

"Ghost – we can call Mrs. Sharpe Whitey," he says (Mrs. Sharpe has blond hair).

"Hey, Mr. Arnold, want some of my chocolate bar?" Jeffrey Swift asks me on the bus trip home.

"Want some of my candy?" asks Ghost quickly. Whenever I ask myself why I'm riding home on a bus on a Saturday night with a group of eight-year-old hockey players, one or two kids usually tell me, in their own little way.

That Saturday night the Leafs whip the Habs. Our telephone rings.

"Hey, Mr. Arnold, how about those Leafs kickin' your Habs' butts!" shouts Curtis Perry.

"Hey, Curtis," I say to him, "they're just trying to finish last this year to get that first draft pick, they're looking way ahead."

"Sure, Mr. Arnold, sure." I can hear his father laughing in the background. My daughter and wife are laughing, too.

I don't know if I can take another Habs loss. Our team is really on me, and even Colin, who used to be a Habs fan, has left them. They tease me about the loss to the Leafs. I can only tell them the Habs must be bad . . . "the Leafs beat them."

Steve and Greg come home from Calgary on the "red-eye." Steve has had only one hour's sleep. He could have stayed in Calgary, but his commitment to his family and team shine through today.

Today we're playing Richmond Hill, a new team for us and one none of us has seen in action yet. We know the coaches are young and energetic, though. We have a short talk with our team in the dressing room, asking players where they should be if the puck is in their own end. We let the players tell us and they have it right. I go through the options. I ask them what they can do once they have the puck out of our zone, and they answer, "Skate with it, dump it, go wide, deke, make a move, shoot, or pass." The kids know them all now. We've come a long way.

"These are your options. You have to decide what is best for the team," I remind them. I also mention that I want them to carry their own equipment, not let mum, dad, or their siblings do it. Some kids have been losing their equipment so I also remind them it's their responsibility to check their bags before they come to the rink.

We have finally come up with a team cheer. Woody is responsible: "We're maroon. We're white. We're dynamite. We shoot. We score. We fight, fight, fight!" It's based on an old cheer used by many teams over the years. But the kids like it so much they troop out of the dressing room, singing it proudly.

We also try a new routine that one of my old teams used. I show it to the team before the game starts. Half the team gets in line with the goalpost and faces toward centre ice; the rest line up on the other side facing each other. One player skates around the net twice, while the other players smack their sticks on the ice, then the skater zooms into the middle of them. They all yell, "Petes!" and skate to centre ice to shake the other team's hands.

The game is quick. At one point one of our coaches has finally done what we don't want to do. Greg yells for a player to pass. It's the first time this year but he instantly recognizes his mistake.

"Sorry, Teak," he says with a rueful grin.

Woody gets a marvellous goal, a backhander in the top left corner. "Mats Sundin couldn't have done that any better," Steve says to me and says the same to Woody when he comes off the ice. Jeffrey Swift makes an excellent pass to Missile, who breaks in on the goalie and makes a skilful deke to score.

"Hey coach, I was wide open and Jeffrey didn't pass it to me," Rocket complains.

"Did you yell for it?" I ask.

"Yeah," he says. I give him a look. He looks right back at me. "Now tell me the truth," I say.

"No, I didn't," he concedes, smiling to soften the admission. He'll yell the next time, though.

Many of our defencemen want to play forward. That's a problem I've created by playing them everywhere. I have to find a way to make defence as much fun as forward. I move defence to forward again. I don't know if it has worked or not, but I know our players can play any position well – we get our first league shutout: a 4–0 victory.

"Whenever our team gets a shutout, we should all be proud," I tell the players after the game. It's good to see them applaud themselves. Maybe I can get the defence to feed off this.

As the players pile out of the dressing room, Greg and I stand in the hallway watching them. It's amazing – just one hour after I've told them to carry their own equipment, six players walk by us without their stick and bag. Mum or Dad have taken it for them.

Colin has already come up with a solution, though – he walks by us with wheels on his equipment bag and instantly a new nickname is born.

"Hey, Wheelsie, good game today," I call. He looks around, smiles, catches his mum's eye, and we know he loves the new nickname.

—✺—

Whew! Riding in a bus full of children can surely have its moments. The gas that some of those bodies emit is sometimes unbearable. Greg and I are smothering our noses tonight as the activity bus heads up Highway 115 to the 401 . . . someone let one riiiiiiiiip!

It's snowing. Road conditions are slippery. The kids' heads are whipping around, looking out their windows – we pass at least four car accidents. One car has landed on its roof.

"Should we be travelling tonight?" asks Greg.

"This is nothing like some nights," I assure him. We won't have to tell the kids to stay in their seats. Greg isn't used to travelling this way. Tomorrow he leaves for Ottawa, then goes to Colorado for a Saturday night game, then to New York for an afternoon game. He's a busy man and travels first-class all the way . . . but not tonight. Tonight we are packed into the bus like sardines, restless sardines.

Earlier, Manager Sharpe had told the parents we would be stopping at McDonald's on the way home from the game. Wrong! She's a good manager but like all managers needs to remember to get things approved by the coaching staff before making team moves. Now I tell the parents, "My buses don't stop on the way home." Many of them are relieved. The kids won't like it, but stopping wastes time and costs money. Besides, it's a school night.

We get to the rink safely and in plenty of time. Our pre-game talk again focuses on options. Every game, more hands go up as they become more confident with their answers. That confidence also begins to show on the ice. Woody leads the cheer for the team and they sing it as they leave the dressing room: "Maroon and white. We're dynamite. We shoot. We score. We're out of sight." Or something like that. Greg says, "I don't have a clue what they're saying but they're looking happy."

Before the game I pull a gumball that I got from a machine at the rink out of my pocket. Missile spots it and asks, "First goal gets it, Mr. Arnold?"

"Okay."

"What about the first save?" asks goalie Mitch.

"Whatever." All I wanted to do was chew it.

The game starts with the usual handshaking at centre ice, except tonight Wheelsie slides right into the opposition's line, knocking several players down. Laughing, the referee gives the baseball umpire's "safe" signal. It did look like a nice slide at home plate. The Whitby coach isn't impressed. To each his own.

On the first shift, Whitby has a two-on-oh breakaway. Mitch makes a great save. At the whistle he looks over to me and shouts, "Keep that gumball for me, Mr. Arnold." Halfway through the game, our goalies switch. Mitch comes out.

"Good game, Mitch," I say to him.

"Where's that gumball, Mr. Arnold?"

Whitby takes a 2–0 lead in the third period. Michael Hickey moves to forward for this game and scores for us – his first goal of the season. Wesley is on the bench again, showing me his tongue-can-touch-the-tip-of-his-nose trick. Our team plays well only for the last six shifts of the game, but fights back to tie it.

We work on that in the post-game talk, telling them how proud we are that they never quit. We make it a point to always find a positive message for them. I just hope they pay more attention to what we say in the dressing room than it seems they did on the bus.

"Hey, we're going to McDonald's," says one player excitedly.

"No, we're not," says Ghost. "Mr. Arnold's bus doesn't stop." The kids grab a piece of pizza or some popcorn at the rink for the bus ride home.

"Hey, Mr. Arnold, can I play forward again?" asks Michael when we're settled on the bus.

"We'll see."

"Hey, Mr. Arnold, can I play forward?" asks another voice. Whose voice is that? I turn, hoping it's not who I think it is. It is: Gloves Millen.

"I'll let you play forward next month," I tell him. He looks at me as if the marbles just fell out of my ears: "I don't want to play in a game, I'm a goalie."

"Hey, can I play goal?" asks Jonathan.

"If you can find equipment, you can play goal at the next practice."

"Nah," he replies. "I'm not a goalie."

"These trips are awful," Greg complains.

"As if you'd know, it's only your second bus trip," I say. We're going to reduce his full-time coaching salary to part-time – but how do you subtract nothing from nothing?

"Hey, Dad," shouts Charlie. "I can't find my shoe."

"It's *your* shoe," replies Dad, who turns to me to ask, "Why would he have his shoe off?" I think of Steve's favourite eye-rolling Millen line – "Goalies!" – but decide to keep my mouth shut.

Bartman has a bloody nose from an elbow to the face. On this team you have to keep your head up on the bus. There's more danger of getting an elbow (or shoe) here than on the ice. As usual, Bill Gillam looks after it.

Before getting off the bus, we make sure every player picks up the garbage from the bus. Then I say to them, "I was going to take you all to McDonald's tonight, but your parents said not to." The kids groan. "Actually, Mr. Millen didn't want to." More groans. In a truly puzzled tone, Charlie asks his dad, "How come you didn't want to go to McDonald's?" Greg throws me a look and says, "Thanks a lot." You're welcome.

Just when you think there are no bright minds left in minor hockey, along comes someone who awakens you to the sheer genius of the game. Steve's patience in practice is admirable. He's a no-nonsense guy who gets his message across without hollering. It's always amazing to look at that clock and see the practice is almost over. It's a sign of a good practice when kids and coaches don't know it's time to leave the ice.

Our next game is a return trip to Richmond Hill. Many of the parents are playing cards in the back of the coach. The kids are up front with the coaches watching a movie . . . *Mighty Ducks 2*. The coaches are reading newspapers and peeking at the movie now and then. Steve and Bill are on board today.

The hockey conversation by the kids, as usual, is about who is going to be captain and assistants and what positions they will play. I talk to every player today, asking them what their favourite position is. Only four of them pick defence as the top choice. Well, I did want them to get to play every position, but I had hoped eventually the kids would enjoy certain positions and start asking to play there. Most of them did, and it was forward.

But I'm never left alone to ponder the principles of coaching for long. "Hey coach, how do you like my hair?" asks Rocket. He has it close-cropped and dyed blond on the top, but dark on the sides.

"Are you getting a lawyer?" I ask.

"What for, coach?"

"You're going to sue the barber, aren't you?"

He lets out a big laugh. "Quit kiddin', coach."

"It looks great, Rocket," I assure him. Hairdos are very popular on this team. C. P. always has his hair slicked forward and pointed at the top, held in place with gel. Wheelsie, even Nathan, are doing the same thing. We make a point of commenting on all their styles.

Rocket is really adapting to this hockey. His personality is opening up, he's talking and participating more. He's also our leading point-getter. We credit much of the progress the team is making to the fact that he's gaining more confidence.

We arrive at the rink almost an hour and a half before game time. The kids watch a game while we wander around the rink. During the pre-game talk, I remind Wesley that the puck goes up the boards in our own end. "Where did you lose it the last game?" I ask.

"Going up the middle," replies Wesley shyly.

—⚶—

The Richmond Hill coaches were Mike DePellegrin and Steve Donegan, two young men in their twenties who were coaching minor novice for the first time. They didn't have any of their own children on the team. Last year they had coached the AAA bantam team – fifteen-year-olds – and found the kids weren't listening. Mike is a communications officer at St. Michael's College. He had found the bantam players "didn't want to be there." He went on, "Hockey didn't seem to be fun for them any more. They weren't enjoying it. The only way a kid at fifteen is going to keep playing is if it's fun, but I think they were playing because they thought they had to. None of them play pickup hockey or pond hockey any more. As a coach I wanted to be somewhere where we could make a difference." He and Steve decided to move down to the minor novice level.

The bantam age has the biggest drop-out rate in Canadian hockey, while the novices are seeing an increase. Mike and Steve's coaching philosophy was like ours – to "forget about wins and losses, and just have fun." But they added, "We wanted to make sure we competed and tried our hardest every night." Because of their philosophy, they didn't have any specialty teams and concentrated on basic skills at practice.

"We only had one goalie. We'd started with two, but the other goalie's parents pulled their kid out before the first game because of rumours among parents that he wouldn't be playing much. They just pulled him out and didn't give us a chance to say anything. We were going to use him." He does admit to shortening their bench at times if the kids weren't trying hard enough. "At the end of the year they had to earn their ice."

The coaches found the league "extreme." "Some teams and coaches were ultra-competitive and you knew the kids weren't enjoying it. We stood in the hallways after one game and listened to the other coach yelling at the players, and we understood why the kids in bantam weren't having fun. We didn't see some coaches ever smile."

Mike had also coached high school hockey, where parents seldom went to the games. "There is no parent element. We have to find a way to make it fun now so it's fun later. Some coaches are taking it too seriously. We played Markham once and we almost tied them. Some of their players came out of their dressing room [after they won] crying."

This year, Richmond Hill didn't win many games. They finished in last place, in fact, but the coaches said they would be back, they had so much fun. According to Mike, the worst thing was the frustrated parents. "They thought their kids would be drafted out of minor novice, and we had to keep telling them the kids were only eight. During some practices the parents would walk right onto the ice and tell their kids, who were leaning on their sticks, not to do that. I know it's AAA but the kids *are* only eight."

—⁓—

Jim Parcells is a former Peterborough Petes trainer who has also worked for the Guelph Storm and the OMHA. He became director of hockey operations for a minor hockey association near Toronto. During his three years in the OMHA he has found that "many parents feel there is some sort of 'pot of gold' at the end of the hockey rainbow that involves a huge signing bonus, a hockey-card contract, and their son's action figure on Sega

Genesis video games." Jim knows the chances of that happening aren't good.

He wrote his college thesis on minor hockey players in Ontario and reading it brings home just how difficult it is for a kid to make it to the NHL. In 1991, Jim looked at 30,000 Ontario minor hockey players born in 1975. Of those players, 232 were drafted to junior A teams. Only 105 of them ever *played* a junior game. Of these 105 players, 90 finished three or four years in the OHL; 42 played NCAA Division I Hockey and very few graduated; 48 of the 30,000 players were drafted by NHL teams, and 35 of those signed with the NHL teams. Only 26 saw any NHL action, and about 15 of them earned a second contract with an NHL team. That's out of 30,000 kids! And before the big European invasion. Interestingly, his research showed that 60 per cent of players who were drafted never played AAA hockey.

What concerns Jim the most is that many parents "will read this and truly believe that their kid will buck the odds and be one of the 'fortunate' dozen-or-so players."

—⁓—

The Richmond Hill game is fun. The coaches don't take the game too seriously. We win 6–3.

Bartman puts on a clinic. He scores a goal along the ice. He scores one from the side of the net, scores one in the top corner, and dives after a puck to slip it by their goalie.

"Hey, you should buy me a pop, coach," he says after his fourth goal. He's chortling.

"You should buy us one for letting you on the ice," Steve and I shoot back.

Bill tries to pull that changing-goalies-on-the-fly trick again. Charlie has skated to the bench, Mitch has left the bench, and the puck is going down the middle of the ice toward our empty net. Ghost picks it off to save the goal and "our bacon."

"That doesn't happen, again," I tell Bill, who apologizes. (We laugh about it on the bus ride home.)

Bartman's line with Nicole and Riley gets ten points. They are buzzing all over the ice. Coppo has his best game of the season, rushing, passing, backchecking, and, in the middle of the second period, he makes my proudest moment. He has the puck in our own zone. Two players are coming at him. He heads up the middle, stops – I can almost feel him thinking, "Oh, oh, not up the middle" – turns, and takes the puck up the boards. Bartman's four goals are nice, but Coppo's move is just as nice.

His dad tells me that Wesley is enjoying himself but he wishes Wes would watch more hockey on television. Many of the kids don't watch hockey on television any more. There are so many distractions. When we were kids, we had one television. It was in the living room. We got one TV station and we all watched *Hockey Night in Canada* together. That's not happening much today.

After the game we talk about how one line worked so hard for all the game, while the others worked only part of the game. We also mention Coppo's play. We never criticize any individual, but we do compliment individuals to try to increase their confidence.

On the bus ride back, Steve and I go over our lineup. I want to start putting kids in more permanent positions. The more I think about it, the more I know we need to get them comfortable and confident in their positions. I'll still switch them up the odd time. Some kids will be disappointed, but they can't all be centres, their favourite position. Steve agrees.

We're home by 6:30, not bad for a Saturday night.

—m—

Today we have an at-home game, against York Simcoe. Last time, they defeated us 5–2, so I'm looking forward to this matchup. I think it will be a good test to see if our team is improving.

During the pre-game discussions, we talk about how hard the one line worked yesterday. We want three lines working today. I also talk about how well the defence has been playing and reminded them not to panic. One of the things you see so frequently in hockey is how hard a team works for the puck and then gives it up so easily by just trying to slap it out. If you have time, take your time, don't just get rid of the puck, we tell the players.

Johnny is here today as well as Steve and Bill. We play a good game. Bill is keeping track of the defence pairings, and today they change almost forty times. We win the game 8–3; it's a game with some interesting features.

Ghost has the puck in our zone and is almost ready to dump it. He doesn't, though; he carries it when he sees the open ice. Two players finally go after him in the neutral zone but he makes a pass, resulting in a goal. I love to see this – a player thinking about what he's doing and making good decisions – more than the goals. The Ghost had a super game, as did Coppo, who is getting more focused every day.

Before the game I had a chat with Nathan because he seems to lack confidence. I told him he should skate as hard in the game as he does in practice. Bingo! He gets two goals by working hard. I'm a genius. He approaches me after the second goal, probably (I think to myself) to say I was right, but instead he grins and says, "Steve [Larmer] is good luck."

"Why is that?" I ask.

"He told me Sherwood sticks will get me more goals," he replies.

Everyone seems to be working harder today. Maybe the "Buzz Line" (Batman, Nicole, and Woody) working so hard yesterday got the other lines going. Ryan is coming off the ice patting his teammates on the back. It's the kind of game that makes you glad you're coaching minor hockey.

The York Simcoe coaches have the right idea. We don't hear them yelling at the kids, and they're playing every one of them, although they don't have seventeen players, so some players get out more often. I still think they are the best team we've played. They just had a bad game today. But everyone wins in a game like today's.

"Hey, Mr. Arnold," Ghost says when he comes off after one shift. "The ref says we're playing like the Leafs, but I told him we're playing like Montreal."

Mitch plays well in net for his half, allowing one goal. When he comes off I ask him what his most difficult shot was and he replies, "The one I let in."

Steve is having fun on the bench, too. He directs the kids patiently, but he also tells them how much their plays are appreciated. Bill is catching on to it as well. Praise is the name of the game. In the post-game talk we tell them how proud we are of their work ethic and remind them what happens when they keep their feet moving.

"Those kids are sure having fun," parent Dave Baker comments as we leave the rink. Me, too.

Today we have a power-skating coach in to work with the kids, so Steve, Greg, Bill, and I go upstairs to the warm room where the parents sit watching. Some coaches try to avoid parents, even leaving the rink through the rear doors. Why? Well, there is a history of hockey parents approaching coaches with suggestions, ideas, and even demands. This team is full of good parents – indeed, most teams are.

Before the kids go on the ice, I tell them it's power skating today.

"Oh no, I think I'm sick," yells one kid as they all moan together.

"I can already skate, so I guess I don't have to,"Wheelsie says again, as he always does at power skating. I remind them the only thing they can do in hockey that doesn't require skating is sitting on the bench. It's a good skate, almost fifty minutes of backward skating. The kids work up a great sweat.

In the dressing room, after the skate, Coppo says, "Hey, Mr. Arnold, look how fast I was skating." He shows me the huge hole in the heel of his sock. "Burned a hole right through my sock."

Gord Sharpe teases his son, "You could use a few holes in your socks." He's amazed at the quality and quantity of equipment available for the kids today. I look around the comfortable dressing room at all the kids and parents. I think of "Red" Sullivan strapping on his skates, sometimes in a blizzard, sometimes with bonfires burning near where they changed into their skates. Many of the Depression-era kids wore clothes made from Quaker Oats sacks. They would search a dump for Bee Hive hockey pictures, bottles, and rags to sell.

"We'd wear our clothes until they wore out," says Red's old-time friend Herb Heffernan. Red's sister, Mary Simmonds, says, "We were warm, had lots to eat, but we didn't have money for extras. There was no television, no electronic games, only magazines, newspapers, and radios to keep informed of the day's events. Parents didn't hardly pay any attention to the kids playing sports in those days."Things have changed, but as I listen to the banter, the chuckles of the kids, I know that one thing never has to change . . . the love of playing a game.

After practice Greg tells the kids that they so impressed us we're going to have power skating again Thursday. Moans, moans, and more moans . . .

—⁂—

The next night our home phone rings. It's one of the parents, who says, "I don't want to be a party-pooper, but some parents were drinking beer on the bus and I don't think that's right with eight-year-old children on it." In response, I write the following letter:

> I have received a parental complaint about the consumption of alcohol by other parents (not coaches or any team officials) on the team bus. Following is the guideline from the Peterborough Minor Hockey Council (PMHC):
>
> "No coach or any other team official will consume alcohol while coaching or travelling to a game involving his team. . . .
>
> "Coaches are responsible for providing each player's parents with conduct guidelines, knowing that they will be ultimately responsible to the PMHC for any complaints received from team members, parents, or officials of any other hockey association where their team is involved. The PMHC recognizes that controlling parents' actions is not possible. However, the coach is expected to provide a positive influence."
>
> I can assure you that no members of our staff have, or will, consume alcohol on the bus.
>
> I can't control the actions of adults, nor would I dare to take that role. However, it is my responsibility to act on a parent's complaint and let all adults know of his/her concern. Thank you.

At the next practice I hand out the notices to coaches and parents. Some parents are obviously sour about it. I didn't sign on to babysit the adults, so they will have to decide what happens next. Some parents want to know who complained. I can't reveal that, adding that it is the kids who are my concern. (I was never aware of what the parents as a group made of the memo and what they decided to do about it. The issue seemed to go away.)

—〰—

"Missile" has a finger wrapped in bandages.

"I got it stuck in a pencil sharpener," he explains proudly. Now, that's an unusual one. "I'll be all right, though," he assures me, but adds, more ominously, "I don't know if I can shoot." After stepping on the ice, he starts to skate away slowly.

"Did you cut your legs?" I ask, wondering how a cut finger can make him skate so gingerly. He laughs, gets the point, then blasts away.

Steve has introduced a new flow drill involving speed, the puck, and passing. Greg wonders why Steve is using two of the "weaker" defencemen to start a new drill. He's afraid they will slow the drill down. And indeed, the drill does start slowly. However, we've learned to be patient when introducing a new drill. A few minutes later everything is going smoothly. The next time we use it will be a lot easier. When I ask Steve why he used those two defencemen, I am pleased with his answer: "We're an inclusion, not an exclusion, team. Everyone should be included."

The banter in the dressing room after practice is about the Habs' three-game winning streak. Now the Habs can have their own Web site because they have three wins in a row: www.

6

Just a Game

"Don't sacrifice a normal family lifestyle trying to turn your nine-year-old into a pro." That's what Jim Parcells preaches to parents. Has any minor hockey coach gone an entire year without a parent problem? Usually we hockey parents are good, normal people, but when hockey and our children are involved, it can be an awful experience.

Some parents think minor hockey should be a school for their child, a place to learn how to play positional, structured hockey, just like they do in the pros. Our team was no different. I knew there would be some problems and there would be parents who disagreed with our coaching style. It was bound to happen and it did. One night before practice two fathers approached Greg and told him they didn't think the kids were learning anything.

"The only people being coached are the goalies," said one parent. Greg listened to these fathers – he missed about fifteen minutes of our practice to hear them out. When he got on the ice, he told me about it. I decided this was something to be dealt with immediately. I didn't want it going any further.

I went to the dressing room, took off my skates, and called a parents' meeting upstairs with whomever was there. It was insulting to Steve that people were saying only the goalies were learning anything. What rink had they been at during practices? Greg and Bill instructed the goalies. Steve and I had the rest. I told the parents that if they didn't like the coaching on this team, and it was incredible if they didn't (me, I could understand, but the rest were all excellent coaches), they could take their child to another team. There was still time in the season to do this. None of them took advantage of the opportunity, either then or later. The discussion went on, and I'm ashamed to say I lost my temper (not a smart thing, but appropriate at times).

One father commented that parents can ask teachers questions about their children, so they should be able to ask coaches about them too. Fair enough – but only up to a point. Teachers are paid for their full-time jobs. Coaches in minor hockey do what they do for the love of the kids and hockey – they don't get paid. Parents pay for ice time, registration, bus trips, but they don't pay the coaches. Nevertheless, we take our responsibilities seriously. We know that thirty-four other unpaid coaches (parents) are usually watching every move. Ask a teacher how he or she would feel if all the parents assembled to watch their kids during classes.

I reminded the parents that we had outlined our philosophy before tryouts, after tryouts, and still . . . we had complaints about the very things we had discussed. But not one parent had said their kid wasn't having fun. This criticism sometimes makes non-parent coaches want to become ex-coaches. But for me, it made my resolve stronger. We would get on with the fun part of the game and the lessons you can learn from hockey. I apologized to the parents for losing my temper. Because, after all, there's so much more to life for these young children than hockey . . . a Santa Claus parade, for example.

Our team had entered a float in the Peterborough Santa Claus parade, which was being held on December 1. I was a float judge with, obviously, one big conflict of interest, so it was decided I couldn't ride with the team – I had to be with the other judges. So it was that on a bitterly cold night all the kids on the minor novice Petes were on the float, along with Steve and Bill. I was inside a warm local restaurant with a window facing the street the parade came along. The float went by and Steve, clearly cold and jealous, spotted me. I waved at him.

A trip to Markham to play the only undefeated team. Batman is sick on the way to the game, so he sits in the front with me. We play horses and cows. The rules are simple. If we pass horses, I get to count them; if there are cows, he gets to count them. We lose our counts if we pass a cemetery. I am leading 30–0 when we pass a cemetery. Batman starts to feel better.

"I've never seen Batman sick," I tell him, and the big smile on his face is enough for me. I tease him about the other times he was sick and got so many points. It all seems to make him feel better.

"Hey, Eddie," says Nicole, looking up from the bench at the arena as the kids are preparing for the game, "I've got the cramps." How do I answer that one? I don't, but ask her during the next shift how she is. She's fine. So am I.

When we're losing 5–3, one of our players, who is on the bench, looks at the clock, which shows more than eight minutes left in the game. Dejectedly, he says, "We can't win now." If we think we can't, we won't.

"The nets are bigger in Markham," both Charlie and Mitch report following the game. It seems the measurements are different only at our ends of the ice, though. We lose 7–3.

Steve puts it to the team this way: "We just had a bad day at the office – sometimes we have those." I tell them a bit more. I remind them to work as a team, to talk with their teammates, to not give up, and to stay on their feet.

"How many players does it take to make this team?" I challenge them. "Seventeen," they yell in unison. We, as a coaching staff, knew Markham would be good. Once before we'd been down 3–0 and tied the game late in the second period, so now we emphasize that positive note. Batman scored one of our goals tonight. In the three times he's been sick he has collected nine points. Stay sick, kid.

While winning isn't what our coaching philosophy is all about, we can't let seventeen kids know this. After all, they play the game to win. Never mind, the kids all got pizza and Gatorade today.

I learned later one father isn't happy with the player we have his son partnered with. "He's not learning anything playing with him," he told Steve. He didn't realize that most of his conversations got back to the other coaches. After all, we were in this together. We thought he should lighten up. We wondered if we should switch partners to make him happy but we kept these thoughts to ourselves – we also didn't change our approach.

I had been waiting for the Markham game, knowing it would be a challenging one. Markham has only two lines and some excellent players, and those excellent players get to play a lot. But my faith in human nature is restored a bit. Other parents must have heard about the whining and many of them called to express their support and remind us that only a minority of the parents complain.

—⚬⚬—

At today's practice we retest the kids, using the same drills we used in their first practice in September. We wanted to compare the results of the two practices. It goes well. I spend a few hours tonight figuring out team averages and individual improvements. All the players have improved. The weaker players, in particular, have improved by giant leaps.

I prepare the following report for the parents:

Minor Novice Petes 2000–2001
Comparative Evaluation

We believe the team has improved in most areas in the first three months of the season. The evaluations seem to support this. We believe the team is thinking more, using teammates more often, and the kids are having fun coming to the rink. We're really pleased with where they are at this point in the season.

We're also happy to note the team evaluation averages have improved in all areas as shown below. The chart shows their times in the drills they did at their first practice on September 5. That drill set a benchmark; we timed them again on December 5 with the same drills.

Team Averages:
Up and back power skate with puck

Sept. 5	15.11 seconds
Dec. 5	14.58

Six cone puck drill

Sept. 5   18.74 seconds

Dec. 5   17.75

Crossover full ice

Sept. 5   23.52 seconds

Dec. 5   21.80

Cone and back

Sept. 5   27.7 seconds

Dec. 5   20.5

We end the report by thanking the parents for their support, positive attitude, patience, and for allowing the kids to play the game. We also thank the players for their enthusiasm in pursuit of team development.

We are also happy to see that the kids are successful in school. They all had excellent report cards. I'm beginning to believe there is something to the Statistics Canada study that found that of 23,000 children and teens studied across Canada, those who were in sports and clubs after school did better in the classroom. They also have higher self-esteem and better social skills than those who don't participate.

—◊—

At this practice, we begin meeting with each player and a parent, or both parents, if they're available. During the interviews we thank the parents and encourage them to continue their support. I ask the kids if they remembered trying out and how difficult it was to make the team. Then we tell them how glad we are they did make the team, how proud we are of them, remind them that the team has improved, that they have worked so hard, and we are proud they were listening, learning, and taking chances.

—m—

We rarely play a Saturday home game – Sunday is our usual home date. But today, a Saturday, we are playing at home and won't be playing at all tomorrow. We're playing Clarington, a new team for us.

It's one of the best games of the year. After two periods the score is 0–0. Mitch makes a spectacular glove save.

"That's probably the save of the year," proclaims a wide-eyed Missile.

"The TSN highlight of the night," I agree.

Gloves goes in halfway through the game. In the third, we take a 1–0 lead on a nice goal by Nicole, who shoots the puck along the ice and into the corner.

"Good low shot, Nicole, right along the ice where the goalie can't see it," I tell her when she comes off.

"My dad taught me that one," she says proudly.

"He's a genius," I remark.

"I know," she says confidently.

One of our defencemen smothers the puck in our crease, and Gloves has to face a penalty shot. It was either that or let the other team score. I've never seen a penalty shot in minor novice hockey before. Clarington scores and later adds another goal on a screened shot along the ice.

Their coach, Gary Moore, runs his team along the same lines as we do. He congratulates us for a well-coached game.

"That was the best game we've played all year," Steve says. We were passing, skating, and checking. Two of our players were missing with illnesses so we made two defencemen wingers and went with four defencemen. Everyone played well. Woody and Jonathan almost scored with fewer than thirty seconds to play. Woody put the puck over the net again.

"I can't stop those field goals," he says after the game, tears running down his cheeks. We tell him he should be proud that he had so many chances.

—⁂—

At today's practice we work on five-on-twos for the first time in more than a month. The kids aren't doing it well so we leave it alone, but otherwise the practice is excellent. In spite of the fact we had twenty-six centimetres of snow fall in a twelve-hour period, winds were gusting at seventy kilometres an hour for a wind-chill factor of thirty-two below (Celsius), only one kid didn't make it to practice. And the weather actually had nothing to do with his absence – he was sick.

Mitch tells me he has something for me after practice.

"You're really going to like it," he promises. And he's right – I do like it. It is a Montreal Canadiens puck. I show it to the rest of the team and say, "Here's what a great team uses."

Most of them boo me and begin to chant, "Leafs, Leafs, Leafs." Only Nicole, Josh, and Ghost shout "Montreal!" Oh well, you can't teach them everything.

—⁂—

"Hey coach, I got my tooth pulled today," shouts Rocket.

"How are you going to eat steak?" I respond.

"I'll chew it on the other side," he retorts.

"Hey Mr. Arnold, look at my tooth." Batman grins and pushes his tooth up to his gum. Why do kids do that?

—⁂—

"Hey, do you think you could find Santa a drink? Anything cold. A beer would be nice," requests an obviously desperate Santa Claus. He's just had seventeen children, one after the other, on his knee, as well as Coach Arnold.

We held our Christmas party in a Peterborough bowling alley. The kids enjoyed the bowling – it was a great way to socialize. Earlier in the day, the kids had been all over the city soliciting donations for the team and raising more than $1,300. Oh – we all received Petes hockey ties for Christmas.

—⁂—

The rivalry game. Peterborough teams have a thing about playing Oshawa teams. It dates back decades, to when the Petes and Oshawa Generals used to have brawls, play close games, and draw plenty of fans whose emotions ran high. Today, we play Oshawa at home.

"Our last game of the year, guys," I say to the kids. They all laugh and say it's not over yet. It takes a while to explain that I mean the year 2000. We don't play another game until 2001. I'm not sure they get it.

We don't have our full complement of coaches – Bill is at a Raptors game in Toronto – but Steve and Johnny are here. So is Greg, who caught the red-eye back after covering a game in Vancouver.

I have finally accomplished something I've tried to do all year . . . beat Steve to the rink. I've done it twice in one week. I beat him to practice Thursday. I had to get there a full hour and fifteen minutes before the practice to do it. He got there ten minutes later. Today I was there two hours before game time.

Greg isn't happy with the Oshawa coach because he pulled one of the goalies after the kid let in a few goals. Greg, who is really concerned that kids not be emotionally damaged by their involvement in sport, wants to talk with the coach and point out that his actions "may hurt the kid all of his life." We advise him to leave well enough alone.

Our team plays well. It's our best positional game of the year and we haven't been teaching positions. We win 7–3, and, as usual, we spread our scoring around. Also, we're in first place in our division and second in the entire league . . . although we aren't keeping track, right?

Coppo gets his first goal tonight. When we get the puck for him, you'd think Santa had just visited him.

But there is a bit of upset. Woody isn't happy with short shifts. "We can't score if the shifts are that short," he says. This kid wants to play all the time. Steve is trying to shorten the shifts, but our problem is that we are enjoying watching the games so much we sometimes forget changes.

I try to talk to every player after the game. Unfortunately, some parents are in a hurry and come into the dressing room before we're done. Why do they think we close the doors? It is the team's dressing room and what I say is for team members' ears only – even the little players know that.

Oshawa coach Cary Booth has brought along some Steve Larmer hockey cards for him to sign. Cary, a Toronto construction worker, has been coaching minor hockey for five years. This is his first year in AAA hockey.

Most of his parents have been good – "about three-quarters of them." Generally, he says, "I had a great group of kids and parents." He believes in a "team game and not one kid taking the puck up the ice." The team, of which his son is a member, practises twice a week, and is slated to be in four tournaments this winter. Practices are based on clearing the zone, skating with the puck, circle drills, and passing. He doesn't have any specialty teams. Cary has shortened the bench this year, but not very often, doing it "only in more important games."

Like us, he keeps seventeen players on his team, two of them goalies. "It's not right to go with fewer. It doesn't give enough kids a chance," he says, adding, "I try to teach the kids puck-patience." He does direct, and yell at, the players from the bench, but tries to do it "without breathing down their necks."

"I do get upset once in a while," he says, "but the kids are happy and they are full of heart."

—⁂—

The fair-play philosophy is universal in minor hockey in Dartmouth, Nova Scotia. Bill Schipilow, who lives in Dartmouth, was himself a novice – at being the parent of a kid playing minor hockey when his first son joined a novice team.

"I had no idea how minor hockey functioned or how it was organized. My son was seven years old. My role as a parent was to drive him to the rink, help out with the team, if needed, fund-raise, etc. I was green when it came to hockey. However, my expectations were to have my son involved in a fun, safe, positive, recreational activity. He loved playing hockey, and I enjoyed participating in the off-ice activities.

"Two incidents come to mind that made me aware kids' hockey was not a positive experience for some of the players. In one rink, as my son and I were leaving, blocking the exit were two people who were yelling and screaming at each other, toe to toe, using abusive and foul language about the novice game that had just finished. One was a parent. The other person was the coach of the novice team. The parent was upset that the game had been lost and was blaming the coach. We had to wait and listen to this in order to get out the door.

"At another rink I was waiting for the start of one of my son's games. I was walking past a dressing room and could hear a coach yelling and screaming at the six- to seven-year-old novice kids for losing the game they had just finished playing. Many of the kids came out of the dressing room crying. My brief involvement in hockey included other negative incidents such as yelling at officials, players being short-benched, coaches yelling at the kids, parents screaming at the opposing players.

"I saw kids at all levels sit on the bench during games instead of playing their shifts. I saw, and heard, coaches yelling and screaming at the kids (again, at all levels) on the bench for making perceived mistakes on the ice. I saw, and heard, parents yelling abuse at young officials (and again, at all levels). I saw and heard parents yelling at kids after games for not trying hard enough and for making perceived mistakes."

Bill didn't like what he saw and heard and he decided to do something about it. In the summer of 1994 he met with three other concerned parents and "started talking about trying to do something about the negative aspects of the game. The Dartmouth Whalers Minor Association experiences were not unique. Every minor hockey association exhibited similar problems."

They conducted and commissioned surveys and proposed that Dartmouth introduce a fair-play program, a first in Canada. He was surprised when he met some resistance and couldn't understand why some people were against the principles of fair play: respecting the rules, opponents, officials, and their decisions, and having everyone participate and maintain self-control at all times. The answer he and the other parents got was that "fair play may have an impact on winning." Nevertheless, the reform group was able to get the fair-play program introduced in the 1994–95 hockey season. At the end of the season the parents were asked if they wanted the program to continue. More than 80 per cent strongly agreed it should.

Bill can see the positive influence it has had for minor hockey participants. The results in Dartmouth?

- Before the program was introduced, the organization was losing 30 per cent of its officials every year. Now there is a lineup of people wanting to officiate.
- In the 2000–2001 hockey season, not one hockey official left the game because of verbal abuse.
- In the previous ten years the association had won five provincial titles at different levels of play. In the first five years after the fair-play program was introduced, the association won five provincial titles.
- After the second year of the program at the bantam level, the number of suspensions was cut in half.
- The rink staff have seen an improvement in fan behaviour and – interestingly – report that the dressing rooms are left cleaner.

"Fair play is not the panacea for all problems in minor hockey," Bill concedes. "We still have the odd parent losing it. We still have the odd parent abusing an official. We still have the odd coach who short-shifts his bench during a game. But all these problems can be addressed because of fair play."

Dartmouth's fair-play program demands fair (not equal) ice time and respect. It requires parents to take an orientation meeting before their child plays. The coaches must be certified (most Canadian organizations require this). Stricter rules for minor hockey have now been introduced across Nova Scotia. For example, for players from ages four to eight, a minimum of two practices are held for every game played. There is a maximum of twenty games per year with no league championships. Teams can enter a maximum of three tournaments and there can be no championship games, statistics, all-star teams or MVP awards in those tournaments. Teams are not allowed to travel out of province for play. Tryouts are not allowed: players are placed on teams according to chronological age. Parents who don't abide by the rules are banned from the arenas. And the association has made another change: because players miss shifts when one of their teammates is in the penalty box (since they only have four players on the ice while the other team gets to keep playing with five), and because the other teams use power plays playing only certain kids (causing more kids to miss shifts), the association has decreed that teams won't play short-handed during a penalty. The player still serves the penalty, as is only right, but teams do not play short-handed and kids don't miss shifts.

Coaches can still get the players they want on the ice in the last five minutes of a game, but only in games in which winning could get the team to another important game – in other words, during playoffs, tournaments, and final league games.

—🐛—

Christmas is only a few days away and it's hard to get the kids' attention. But never mind, it *is* Christmas.

Today is the day of the Christmas skills contest. I've pitted three teams of five against each other for drills such as speeding around the ice, skating around cones, shooting on net, and relay races. The kids love it. I've kept point totals because next week we'll have a mini team tournament with three teams competing in a scrimmage.

—🐛—

Christmas is two days behind us – whew! Time to get back to some semblance of normalcy. Gloves isn't too happy that we are having a practice today. He was skating on his outdoor rink and had to be dragged to practice. But once he got there, he loved it.

The winning team in our mini-tournament today is told it will get a set of old minor Petes sweaters. These old sweaters had been given to me by a former minor Petes manager, so it gets them out of my garage and gives the kids something to keep as a reminder of the season – they aren't allowed to keep the sweaters they wear during the regular games. Besides, it's Christmas! There are enough sweaters for all the kids, so they all get one at the end of the scrimmage.

The kids are still excited. "That's a smart Santa Claus who came to your house, Ghost." He's wearing a new Montreal Canadiens hat. He gives that big smile of his, but Mitch points out that Santa left Toronto Maple Leafs stuff at his house.

"I know, even Santa has a tough time getting Montreal stuff," I say.

"Hey, Mr. Arnold, I got three watches for Christmas," says Coppo. I reply, "You'll have a lot of time on your hands."

"Really funny."

"Hey, C. P., did Santa come to you?" I ask Curtis. His reply? "He lives at the house." Okay. (He also visits bowling alleys.)

Bill Gillam had to do inventory at work but Greg and Steve are here. I have the week off and get to the rink an hour before practice. Steve is already there. We do a few warm-up drills before the scrimmage.

"Hey, Mr. Arnold." Josh is skating over to me with a concerned look on his face. "My cup fell out of my jockstrap."

Laughing, I say to him, "That's one piece of equipment I won't be helping you with – go tell Mr. Larmer."

Josh laughs back at me: "He sent me over to you." Steve smiles across the ice at me. I tell Josh to go to the players' bench and fix it.

The rules of the scrimmage are the same as any other game except that any penalty will mean a penalty shot. Steve will be the referee.

The idea behind the Christmas scrimmages is for the team to have more fun, but also to show the coaches where weaknesses exist in the units. One unit is particularly hard-working and has taken a 5–1–0 lead over the other two units.

Missile has already given up, saying, "We'll lose." We assure him there is plenty of time (his team later ties the game with only one second left in the practice). The other line doesn't do as well and complains about the referee, jokingly, of course. I think. "Quit your whinin' and start your workin'," says Steve.

It's a great scrimmage, and, because nobody is on the ice after us, we get an extra fifteen minutes. Greg sometimes interrupts the scrimmage to show the defence where they should be.

"He really is Mike Keenan," observes Steve wryly.

We were going to have another practice Friday but I've cancelled it. Why? Why not?

We wish the team well and say again, "See you next year."

"Huh, what's Mr. Arnold talking about?" I can hear them asking one another as I leave the dressing room.

7

JANUARY

Catching the Dream

Hockey tournaments are held all over Canada at all times of the year, but December and January are two of the busiest months for them. Minor hockey organizations set up the tournaments both for competition and as a fundraiser. Tournaments are also great for getting the team together, acting as a little morale booster. Parents either share rides and rooms with each other, or drive to the tournament with their kid and have a room for themselves. Usually at the minor novice level both parents go, but by bantam the parents are happy to pool resources to keep costs down. Some teams have certain rules for players at tournament time. Our only rule was to get plenty of sleep and *enjoy the weekend*!

—ɯ—

Our numbers are down a bit today. Greg has taken Charlie to Ottawa to "bond" while he does the colour commentary for a Senators game. Rocket is home sick with the flu.

We're feeling pretty relaxed after the holidays. Steve and I chat about the Canadian juniors' win today in the World Championships. I'm not impressed by the Canadian team, but what's a minor novice coach know?

In the dressing room, Batman proudly shows me that he has shaved his number 14 in the back of his hair.

"Oh, Batman, too bad," I say to him. "I've decided to change all the numbers around."

"Oh well," his father sighs. "Women change their styles all the time – he can probably change his number." Batman just smiles.

"I lost another tooth, Mr. Arnold," says Mitch. If he loses any more, he'll have to eat Pablum. His aunt had told him if he lost teeth on New Year's Eve, the tooth fairy would bring double the money. He pulled his latest tooth on New Year's Eve.

"Hey, Mr. Arnold," says Nicole. "You know what my dad got for Christmas?" and before I could answer she goes on, "A Rocket Richard sweater just signed by him." Hmmm, interesting, considering that the Rocket is no longer with us. (I ask her father about it later and it turns out to be Jean Béliveau's sweater, but he does have one signed by the Rocket.)

Coppo jumps on the ice with these World Wrestling Entertainment words: "Let's get ready to rumble. . . ." I want to restore some discipline at practice. Lack of attention is a frequent by-product of Christmas and these kids are jumpy. I immediately get two of them who are late to skate a lap. The team starts paying attention as Steve runs through the skating drills. Horseshoes, two-on-ones, passing drills, skating circles, then we'll end it with three-on-three games.

After practice we go to the dressing room. (Coaches get dressed in a separate room but we like to talk to the kids first. Ten years ago, we dressed in the same room, but political correctness has changed all that.) Wheelsie's cousin, who played major novice for a town outside Peterborough, is here. When I ask about his team, he says, "We haven't lost yet."

"We haven't lost all year either," I say.

"Sure we have, coach," says a puzzled Wheelsie.

"Think about it. The year is only two days old." Wheelsie chuckles, shakes his head, and turns to his smiling cousin with a look that seems to say "The coach is an idiot."

We remind the team of the Barrie tournament coming up this Friday. It's our only overnight tournament. Greg, John, Steve, Bill, and I will be there. It might be the first time in a month we've all been together. The kids have already discovered, through the Internet, that the hotel has a swimming pool.

—⚏—

Finland beats Canada in the junior tournament. I call Rocket to find out how he's feeling.

"I'll be able to play in the tournament, coach." That's good enough for me.

I call Johnny to see if he will be able to attend and to let him know we can share my room. He's now our legal trainer. It's taken four months to get his OMHA trainers' certificate approved.

—⚏—

I head to the Barrie tournament tonight. Before Steve and I turn in for the night at the Barrie Travelodge, we have a few cold ones and talk about – surprise, surprise – hockey. We wonder why hotels and motels rarely sponsor minor hockey since they make a great deal of money out of minor sports. A lot of money is made in minor sports in Canada – it's no wonder the Canadian government plays a significant role in promoting it. The government's involvement really started in the 1950s when Canada did poorly in the World Hockey Championships and the Olympics. Members of Parliament were getting an earful about the state of hockey in Canada and the government made a decision then to get more involved.

Studies have shown that children who participate in sports do better at school and are less likely to smoke. Girls are 93 per cent less likely to use drugs and 80 per cent less likely to have an unwanted pregnancy. In Northern Manitoba it has been found that the crime rate decreases by almost 18 per cent in communities that establish sports programs.

Sport accounts for 1.52 per cent of Canada's employment; more than 59,000 people are coaches, referees, or athletes. There are about 600,000 registered soccer players and more than 500,000 registered hockey players, and they have more than 110,000 volunteer coaches with a further 1.8 million people volunteering in other capacities. The Canadian Hockey League draws more than 5 million people every year to its Junior A hockey games.

Every year, Canadians spend more than $2.5 billion on sportswear, more than $2 billion on athletic equipment, $403 million on live sports spectacles, and over $3 billion to use recreational facilities. Of Canada's total gross domestic product, sport accounts for $8.9 billion, or 1.1 per cent. This is almost as much as agriculture, at 1.81 per cent, and exceeds mining, at 1.07 per cent.

Tonight, many hockey families are in Barrie to spend some of this money. Others will arrive tomorrow for the first game at 10:30 a.m.

—⁂—

Our first game will be against Humber Valley. The kids are pumped for it. You can feel their excitement in the dressing room. They are attentive to our pre-game spiel and answer our questions well about their options.

The Humber Valley game turns out to be by far the best game we have played as a team all season. The kids are passing, shooting, checking, backchecking, keeping their heads up, looking for each other, and making the right decisions. Our goalies are walls. We win 2–1, a real team effort, a joy to watch, and well worth the trip.

Watching them play is all we had to do today – the lessons have been taken to heart and their game unfolds as it should. Not everything is so peaceful behind the Humber Valley bench. Some of their coaches are yellers. In the last minute of play, it was as if the Stanley Cup rested on the result. They shortened the bench, yelled directions, and got very excited. After the game, one of the Humber Valley coaches approaches me with some "issues."

"Your parents shouldn't sit behind our bench," he says. He is irritated by their cheering and during the game made sure our parents knew it. When one of our parents shot back at him that he noticed he was "suddenly shortening his bench," the conversation ended. I listened to the Humber coach but didn't respond. He was also upset that the game had gone two ten-minute periods and a fifteen-minute period. The rules were three ten-minute periods. He didn't object during the game, only after it. We spotted the time problem on the score sheet before the game but didn't care – win or lose, our kids would get another five minutes of ice time.

Steve agrees that it was our best game. He was blown away by how well the players were making decisions. If we don't win another game, we know we've seen something special today.

Our next game won't be played until 4:45 p.m., so we eat lunch, go back to the room, and have a light nap. Johnny arrived late last night after attending a Petes game in Peterborough and will miss tonight's game because of another Petes game, this time in Mississauga. He'll drive back to Barrie for Saturday morning's kids' game. He seems to be having fun.

There is more excitement for us. Greg tells Steve and me the CBC is interested in doing a documentary about our team for the special annual program called *Hockey Day in Canada* in February. When Steve and I get back to the hotel, CBC producer Paul Harrington is already calling. The program will feature Steve, the former NHL player, giving back to the community. A CBC crew will travel to a game on our bus, go to a practice, and spend about five days in Peterborough. Steve doesn't want to be the focus of the piece, but agrees it is a great way to get our coaching views out to other Canadians.

We share the exciting news with the parents, and I take the opportunity to tell them about the diary I am keeping. They are as thrilled about the CBC as we are. I'm not sure how they will react now that they know about the diary. Will they become more guarded in their comments? But we want to get our message to other parents, and coaches, so the diary and documentary seem well worth the effort.

Josh thinks his toe may be broken, but his mum says he can still play. He's playing so well, I say maybe he could break his other toe. Johnny says the toe isn't broken but he tapes it anyway.

Our 4:45 game is a half-hour behind schedule. A delay like this isn't unusual in tournaments. Time may be lost because of injuries or for other reasons and, as the day progresses, the delays add up.

A reporter and photographer arrive from the *Barrie Examiner*, the local daily, to do a story about Steve and Greg. The reporter walks up to Steve and asks where he can find them. Steve points to Greg in the dressing room and then walks away smiling.

A parent from another team stops me in the lobby. "Can you tell these young boys who the coaches are on your team? They don't believe me," he says.

"Sure," I reply. "Ed Arnold is the chubby old four-eyed guy. The young, thin guy is Bill Gillam." We all laugh, then I tell the boys about Steve and Greg. Later, the newspaper photographer takes a picture of Steve and Greg on the team bench. We engage in a bit of horseplay – Steve gets on his tiptoes to make Greg look really short(er). I grab Bill and remind the photographer the real coaches are over here. It's neat to think the two old pros still give the fans a thrill.

There is some bad news this weekend, though. Greg confides in me that Roger Neilson, a long-time coach and friend of Peterborough, has been stricken with cancer again. Roger is a strong character, with a deep belief in God. It is this faith that keeps him going. I silently pray for him.

Tonight we're playing Hamilton. We watch them in the warm-ups and can see they're a very good team. Their first shot comes in the first minute but it ricochets off the crossbar.

"Okay goalies, this could be a long one," Greg laughs. Our goalies are up to the challenge. So are our defence and forwards. Rocket is robbed by the Hamilton goalie on a breakaway. He dekes and shoots. The goalie slides on the ice. At the last second, the goalie kicks his leg high in the air and the puck falls back into him. It's the save of the season.

We take a 1–0 lead on a goal by Wheelsie. Then Hamilton scores with forty-nine seconds left in the game. This game ends tied, as it probably should. It was another great game of hockey.

We are amazed at these kids. Steve makes one of his insightful comments on our way to supper: "You know, I wonder how we would have done if the Hamilton coach shared our philosophy instead of imposing that positional play?" He's right. The Hamilton kids played their positions, and played them well, but we felt their freedom and creativity were restricted. We know if the other team had let their dominant players go, we would have been in trouble.

—⁂—

Game time is 7:15 a.m. We're up at 5:30 and on the road at 6:00 for a five-minute trip. "I like to give myself some time to get lost," Steve says.

Johnny is back. He had to drive through a storm in Mississauga at midnight. We need Steve's "lost" time. It takes us fifteen minutes to get to the rink. "We wanted to see a bit of Barrie," we explain to the curious parents. Nice place, Barrie.

The *Barrie Examiner* Saturday edition is on the streets with a positive article about Steve and Greg. It includes a picture with Steve looking so much taller than Greg. Bill and I must be in the next edition. . . .

The kids are ready by 6:50 and want to hit the ice. They have to win to have a chance to advance to the semifinals Sunday morning. We don't tell them this, but they know it. Our opposition is Richmond Hill, from our own league.

Again today, our goalies play brilliantly. We're a bit more scrambly than yesterday but our defence is excellent. The young Richmond Hill coaches conduct themselves well – no yelling or screaming. Their team has come a long way.

"Do we play again if we win?" Wheelsie asks. I can only tell him "maybe," because it depends what the other teams do in their games. We win 2–0, but we won't know if we are in the semifinals until later in the day.

Johnny and I return to Peterborough. If we make it to the semis, I'll come back to Barrie in the morning. Most of the parents go back to their rooms to wait. Within thirty minutes of being home, I get the call from Bill. Good news – we're in.

—⚒—

Amazingly, Steve (who had stayed at his brother's house about a half-hour from Barrie) and I arrive at the rink at exactly the same time: 7:30 a.m., two hours before the game.

We aren't the only anxious ones. Soon the parents are drifting into the rink too. Many of the parents are now calling their kids by their hockey nicknames. Ryan Donohoe even signed the tournament registration sheet as Ryan "Missile" Donohoe. Some of the parents have been in Barrie since Thursday night and will pay more than $350 for their rooms. To keep the costs down, many of them brought their own food, and even toasters.

Our game is against a team from our own league, the ever-dangerous York Simcoe. Greg is here, which is amazing, because he covered the Montreal–Ottawa game last night in Ottawa. Johnny will be travelling with the Petes to Guelph today, but in a move of bold confidence he brought bags of candy to my house last night: "A bag for the win after the first game, and one for after the second game."

We're as ready as we can be. We've seen our team grow this weekend. They are looking for each other, passing, dumping, shooting, hanging on to the puck, using their brains to make excellent team decisions. Today is no different. The game is a dandy – no goals until the third period. Both teams' goalies are playing extremely well in the end-to-end action. Some scoring chances open up for us, but we just can't seem to get the puck in. In the third period, York Simcoe takes a 2–0 lead. Their second goal comes with 3:43 left in the game. It doesn't look good for us.

"Just get the next one, then we'll get the next one and we'll be into overtime," I tell the kids. We tell them not to give up, and they don't. With 2:34 left, Missile beats two players and slides one into their net. Moments later, Woody almost ties it up. Nicole and Batman get a couple of good chances. With barely more than a minute left to play, Steve yells up the bench to ask who we want out for the extra attacker when we pull the goalie.

"Next guy up."

Bill calls out a warning that the next two defencemen may not be the best to put out next.

"Put them out, they all have to learn and be put in these positions." They all agree. We pull Gloves. With twenty-four seconds left in the game, Nathan moves the puck to Woody, who slips it to Missile, and he shoots one by their goalie. It is bedlam on our bench and in our fan area. Our players are jumping and screaming. Steve and I smile at each other as we pat the players, who are cheering from the bench.

Greg starts talking to me about the goaltending for the overtime. Mitch played the first half of the game, Charlie the last half. I don't want to pull Charlie in overtime because putting Mitch back in cold might hurt. Greg says, forget the competition for a minute, he agrees maybe Charlie should stay in, but shouldn't we be fair and put Mitch in halfway through the overtime? Well, if we're going to be fair, Mitch should go in at the start of the ten-minute overtime and Charlie go in halfway through it. Steve, Greg, and I agree on this plan.

Mitch makes an outstanding glove save in the first minute of overtime. So much for coming in cold. It's our first overtime of the year, and for many kids it's the first of their lives. We have plenty of chances but can't bury the puck. York Simcoe's goalie is also outstanding. The period is just more than four minutes old. As usual our team is in their end, defencemen and all. The puck gets out of their zone, and we're chasing a York forward, who scores a nice goal. Mitch doesn't have a chance on it. Our team skates to the dejected Mitch and surrounds him with a hug.

It was a great game to be in, to watch and remember. But our kids are really dejected in the dressing room – some of them are crying, others are hanging their heads.

"That was, and could be, the greatest game in hockey history," I say to them. "I was proud of you guys all weekend. You sweated, worked hard, passed, and made great decisions. Unfortunately, one team has to lose. One team gets to win. This time it was us, but there will always be a next time. Be proud of yourselves. This was a great hockey game."

Steve and Greg back that up. This helps some kids, but not others. Coppo won't look up. It's one of the few times he doesn't have a smile. Every player's hair is "sweat wet." Presently, many of the parents come into the room and praise the kids for the team effort. They are as excited as all of us. Sometimes you have to lose to win.

I go into the York Simcoe dressing room to tell them how well they played and wish them luck in the rest of the tournament. I still think they are the team to beat in our league. Some of their kids come out of the dressing room to get Greg's and Steve's autograph. More kids gather around them. Greg will sign for about fifteen minutes. Steve, as quiet as ever, isn't as easily recognized, though many fathers know him.

Out in the lobby, many of our players are already at the snack bar, laughing and joking. The kids will forget this loss before some of our parents will. We know some parents will feel like us, happy to be involved in a game in which the kids never quit, a game in which they came back and got into a great overtime. Other parents will blame the coaches for the loss and argue that we should have put the strongest players out there. "This is AAA hockey," they will say. "The other team did it." In our minds all the players are strong, they all deserve to be on the ice. If they don't all learn to be in pressure situations now, they'll never get to be in them. We feel good about ourselves. This weekend was well worth the adventure.

The Coppaways are getting ready to pull away in their truck. There's a dream catcher dangling from the rear-view mirror. It's an Ojibwa artifact that has become a best-seller in native stores. The catchers are circular, with a decorative web in the middle; feathers on beaded strips of leather hang from the edge of the circle. Dream catchers have spiritual significance and usually hang in the home. The belief is that the night air is full of dreams. When the air moves freely, it catches dreams floating by. Good dreams find their way through the centre web and slide down the soft feathers so gently they don't disturb anyone. The bad dreams get caught in the webbing and are destroyed when the sun rises. Coppo will have good dreams tonight – although I hear him pleading for "another chocolate bar."

As for me, it's back to Peterborough. I'll be home by 1:00 p.m. – in time to watch the NFL playoffs. Driving four hours for forty-five minutes of hockey may seem silly. It probably is, but all of us will have the memories, and you can't buy those. Halfway home I feel a bulkiness in my coat pocket. Johnny's candies are still there. Mmmm, they aren't that bad.

—w—

During practice, a disappointed C. P. says to me, "Look, Mr. Arnold," and shows me his broken stick. The blade has snapped off the aluminum shaft. We have plenty of spare sticks at games but nobody brings any for practice. I let him use mine.

"You'll have an extra-long reach," I tell him as he skates away. Later little Jessie Gregory, Josh's brother, comes down and hands me his stick for Curtis to use.

Before practice began, I had reinforced the pride generated by the tournament. Steve did the same thing. The kids are a bit tired today, probably because they've returned to school after having been off for two weeks. Charlie is sick and doesn't come to practice but Greg does.

Things get back to normal quickly. Nicole skates by, slaps me on the leg with her stick, laughs gleefully, and skates away. "Hey, Eddie, I can't shoot," complains Swifto (Jeffrey Swift), showing me an injured hand. "You couldn't before," I tease . . . and get a laugh out of him. Wheelsie has some new skates. C. P. is hit and goes down with an injured wrist. It's the first time I've seen him go down all year. He gets back up and skates away with some tears. Later he'll get hit in the neck. "Not a good day, eh, Mr. Arnold?" he says. Nope, but he never stopped.

Steve has them practising their wrist shots and passing today. It gives us time to go around and watch each player.

"I can't shoot," Swifto says, as he winds up and takes an excellent shot. Steve lets them play British Bulldog for the last five minutes of practice. Greg begs off this game. He's still hurting in the ribs from Christmas practice when he had collided with two kids.

Steve is in Pittsburgh for the NHLPA, but Greg is at practice tonight with Bill and me (I have a cold that is growing worse every day).

Greg gets a new nickname today. Before we start I outline the fifty-minute practice that Steve has left behind for us. "I'm going to throw a little loop into that, Teak," says Greg proudly.

"What?"

"You'll see."

"What?"

"You'll see."

We skate away. Maybe he's got a surprise for the kids. Who knows with him? I whistle the kids over, outline the practice, and we're ready to start. But Greg suddenly breaks in: "I'll take the defence down at this end. You've got the other half of the ice." That's quite a loop. He'd be fired in the big leagues. The forwards get half the ice on an unscheduled drill, and he's going to "work on pivots." Steve is right when he says, "Goalies!" From now on, he's "Loops" Millen.

Gradually the players are getting into the habit of bringing their water bottles. There's nothing wrong with the kids having water; they should, but they are leaving their drills to take the drink instead of waiting for scheduled breaks. Anything to avoid work, no matter how old you are. We'll change that.

Other than "the loop," it's a good practice, filled with fun and hard work. We have a shootout near the end. The winners get to go into the dressing room and the losers stay on the ice to do a few laps. The kids love it. We call the last skaters "The Leafs" (another word for losers). Some of the winners planned a water fight for when the Leafs entered the room. It's tough when eight-year-olds act like kids. Sending the winners in first felt like a good idea, but we decide next time to send a coach to the dressing room with them.

—ᴍ—

Most of our games are daytime adventures but this one is another Friday-night adventure. It is played at 7:00 p.m. in Darlington, a small rink near Bowmanville, a thirty-five-minute drive from

Peterborough. Steve's flight lands in Toronto at 4:00 p.m. and he'll meet us at the rink. Loops had to go to Calgary. By 5:00 p.m., Bill and I are on the bus with seventeen kids, but only ten parents . . . mmm, something tells me most of the parents would rather drive their own vehicles than be on this activity bus.

Tonight the roads are clear, the weather is cool. We have music on the bus. A CD player roars out the kids' tunes. Woody, the official team tunes man, plays songs with such titles as "Bawitdaba" and "All Star" by such groups as Prodigy and Smash Mouth – songs and groups that are totally unfamiliar to me. One of the songs has a really good beat and the kids are yelling the words. I can't make out any of the words, but the song gets heads bobbing, even mine.

Steve arrives about ten minutes after the bus. As the kids get dressed and I'm filling out the score sheet in the hallway, that same head-bobbing tune is roaring in the dressing room.

"You know the words to that song, do you, Ed?" Ann Millen asks with that sweet I've-got-something-to-tell-you smile of hers. Oh, oh. Turns out the song was about discovering how to "do it" on the Discovery Channel.

That's enough. The song is banned.

"Oh, but my aunt gave it to me and she has a two-year-old kid," whines Josh, now called "J. G." Yeah, the two-year-old can't sing the words yet.

Rocket, a music lover, runs, with his shoes undone and hockey gear on, out of the dressing room.

"Where're you going?" I shout.

"To get a disk from my mum." These kids aren't focused on hockey tonight.

—ɯ—

The Clarington Toros are a good team, well-coached and tied with us for first place in the division. How do I know we're tied? Parents have gone into the OMHA Web site and printed out the standings. Although Steve and I don't usually have a clue about the positions or stats, the parents, and many kids, do.

Clarington's coach, Gary Moore, is in his ninth year of coaching minor hockey. He has an older son whom he has coached and has a son on this minor novice team. The Toros system is much like ours. They compete in more tournaments, four this year, but they believe in teaching the basics.

"They can learn systems when they're older," says Gary, a title searcher for the City of Toronto. He doesn't like to shorten the bench but admits he does so in tight games, especially in the playoffs. He did it once in overtime, in a playoff game against York Simcoe.

He hasn't had many problems with his parents. "Everything was minor, a few small fires to put out. Some parents like the kids playing evenly and others would rather have two lines," he says. He kept seventeen players, including the two goalies, just like our team. He believes coaches need to "develop the supporting cast." He explains, "The good ones will be good but we always need the supporting cast. You have to make it fun and develop all of them."

Clarington picks their teams in the spring, unlike our late-summer selections. The team doesn't play summer hockey but the parents have an extra couple of months to do fundraising before the season begins. Our similar attitudes probably make the games we play against each other so enjoyable. Gary seldom yells. Some of his assistants do, but he keeps good control of the bench.

Clarington is focused on the game today (they also had music blaring in the dressing room). They get two breakaways in the first five minutes of the game to take a 2–0 lead, but we fight back to tie it. By the end of the first period, they lead 3–2. The second period is more even play. We score three goals, they get two, and the period ends 5–5.

I sit my first kid in this game. He takes two penalties. Because one of them is a flagrant bodycheck in a no-bodychecking league, I have no choice. We can't allow that sort of behaviour, so he sits out one shift. His response? "I don't care, he hit me first." We all must have missed that hit. Guess who? Coppo. (However, after this game he takes fewer penalties. Almost 75 per cent of his penalties were taken before the Barrie tournament.)

Clarington scores on both power plays. We try to explain the importance of not taking penalties and hurting the team and hope it remedies the problem. It may have for Coppo, but Missile takes another two penalties, for tripping and slashing.

There were some marvellous passing plays to set up the goals, with give-and-goes, backhanders – it is wonderful to watch – but the kids don't look like they did in the Barrie tournament. I'm not sure if I'll ever see better novice hockey than I saw on that weekend. With only one minute and thirteen seconds left, Clarington scores the winning goal.

After the game we notice that the kids aren't listening to our little post-game talk. They are tuning us out. Is it the cockiness from the Barrie tournament in which they played so well? Is it playing on a Friday night? Is it that we never yell? Is it because we repeat ourselves? Is it just one of those nights? Is it the music? Is it our imagination? Finally we all agree it's none of the above . . . it's Loops. We would have won tonight, if only he hadn't interrupted practice for those pivot drills. No doubt about it, Loops cost us the game! It's unanimous. Goalies!

My cold won't go away. Combined with the noisiest bus trip in the history of hockey it gives me a major-league headache.

I asked the bus driver how noisy these kids were compared with other teams: "Oh, I don't know, I tune the kids out." I need his tuner. It was a long day, starting work at 7:00 a.m., home at 10:00 p.m., pizza, washed down with a few cold ones, and sleep.

—⚏—

Today's game is against Clarington again. It's Coppo's birthday too, so I jokingly remind him before the game, "You're the oldest guy on the team, so start acting your nine years."

—⚏—

"*You're* the oldest guy," he shouts back. Later in the game he gets a penalty for hooking. Johnny laughs, shakes his head, and says, "Happy birthday, Wes."

This game features action up and down the ice. Batman even gets a penalty shot. The goalie saves it but Steve comforts him, saying, "I had five of them in my career and only scored twice." Having to take a penalty shot puts a lot of pressure on an eight-year-old, just as much as on the goalie, but that's hockey.

During the game Steve mentions to nobody in particular that he forgot his gloves and his hands are cold. How thoughtful are kids? "You can use mine," volunteers Batman, ready to hand him his hockey gloves.

"Thanks, Barts, but I don't want to stink up my hands," says Steve, laughing.

"Hey, Eddy," says Nicole in the middle of the game, "I tore my skin today when I was zipping up my coat."

"Did it hurt?"

"Certainly."

"Did you cry?"

"Certainly, wouldn't you?" Let's get back to the game.

We lose a close one, 4–3, but it was a game well worth being involved in, one of those games that make you want to play another.

—⚬—

Tonight's game is held in nearby Omemee, where a CBC television crew is going to join us to film the documentary on Steve and minor hockey in Peterborough. Steve and I are both nervous about this so we meet with the CBC crew at Steve's house for a couple of hours in the afternoon. They're going to be here for four days. Great. They are also interested in the journal/diary I'm writing. Scott Russell, a CBC announcer, has told them about it. Good. They're interested in interviewing me Tuesday. That's bad.

The crew gets on the bus with us tonight, filming kids and parents. Everyone is great and it turns out to be a lot of fun. This bus was a special activity bus, a yellow forty-four-seater. Some parents had suggested we get a coach, but I thought if it was Canadiana the CBC was after, we'd better let them live it.

At the rink, they come into the dressing room and film our rituals – the team passing the puck around, shouting our chant, and listening to the pre-game talk. Coppo wouldn't keep quiet so I remind him he's going to be on national television. That doesn't stop him.

"He must be from Peterborough," I explain, flustered.

"Hey, I'm from Curve Lake," he shouts.

We didn't know which team would show up tonight but Steve and I were glad the A team did. We win 9–3, but more importantly these kids made plays we had not seen all year: a defence-to-defence pass, a tic-tac-toe goal.

"Even if we lose, those plays were worth the game," says Steve. Loops is at the game, as is Johnny with his candy (the leftover Barrie goodies). Jonathan gets a hat trick and Johnny throws his hat onto the ice.

Greg and I have a great laugh tonight. One kid (he shall remain nameless) comes up to us during the game and says, "I have to go to the bathroom." Before I can reply he adds, "Don't worry, I already went."

Before we can say anything to that, he goes on, "And it wasn't number one."

"You're not serious?" I ask in amazement.

"Either that, or it was the biggest fart ever." We just lose it. What could we do but laugh, keep it to ourselves, and out of the range of the CBC microphones?

The CBC stays with us until we get back on the bus. It has been another long day; home at 9:30. Practice tomorrow, and CBC doing an interview with me.

—◊—

The CBC interview takes hours, for what will probably be a few seconds of the broadcast segment. They tape our practice and equip Steve with a microphone. A cameraman gets on the ice with his skates, surprising both kids and coaches. At our request, they interview every player on our team. Why have we done that? The CBC will pick the ones they want to be aired – better to blame them if someone doesn't appear on television. They also interview some parents. Oh, oh.

"If you're going to talk the talk, we'd better walk the walk," Steve had said before we applied for this coaching job. I think we're doing that.

After practice, Charlie Millen comes into the coach's dressing room while he's waiting for his dad.

"What's wrong, Gloves?" I ask. He looks a bit down. "Did the interview not go too well?"

"It was okay, Teak."

"What did they ask you?"

"They asked me if I liked Mr. Larmer as a coach."

"What did you say?"

"I said he was fine." Then he looks at me with his dark puppylike eyes and sadly announces, "But they didn't ask about you, Teak."

—m—

It's "crackers" day at practice. Steve "has his life back" now that the CBC crew is gone. It was interesting, but we're glad it's over. We'll wait nervously for the airing next month.

Mitch is down on the ice during the warmups.

"What's wrong, M. G.?" I ask, bending over the little lad.

"That got me right in the crackers – guess that's why we wear jocks?"

A few minutes later, Bradley Baker blocks a shot and says the puck "almost hit the crackers." What's with this crackers thing?

One mother asks Steve about her son's play. She doesn't think he is playing as well as he was earlier in the year. We think he's been the most outstanding player for the last three games. Steve assures her he's doing fine. I wonder why she didn't ask *me*? I wonder if it has anything to do with the same player asking me today why he isn't playing centre? Doubtful. I wonder why the passes during the drills aren't as good as they were Tuesday? Maybe these kids need a camera to perform.

There are some discipline problems today. A couple of the kids aren't listening to Steve. I send them around the rink for a skate. They always look at me when they're done; I always smile, and they smile right back.

Steve won't be at the Saturday game in Oshawa. He's taking his daughter Bailey to the Leafs game as a surprise for her. Bailey loves hockey, especially goaltending. Dominik Hasek and Curtis Joseph, two of the best NHL goalies, will be in the nets. I'm surprised that Steve is as excited to be going as he is. Maybe he really doesn't know who he is and what he's accomplished. Greg will be out west. Bill and I will be alone again. People at our game will be looking for the "real" coaches.

—⁂—

On the way to Oshawa for an away game, Ghost says that his friend Fred could play for us today.

"Who's Fred?" I ask, not sure I really want to know the answer.

"He's my friend beside me," says Ghost. There is nobody there.

"He's his imaginary friend, Mr. Arnold," says Gloves. Oh, but of course.

Jonathan "Ferrari" Nauta has motion sickness on the bus so his mum brings him up to sit with me. I call him Ferrari, I tell him, because he's big and strong, just like the car.

"What car?"

"A Ferrari."

"What's a Ferrari?"

I have cut out a picture of the famous sports car from a magazine and brought it to show him. Ferrari and I play the horses-and-cows game while he's sick. I count the animals on my side of the road, he counts them on his; if either pass a cemetery we lose the number, something like the game Bartman and I played earlier in the year. I'm winning 15–3 when we pass a cemetery in Oshawa. Naturally, his motion sickness has disappeared.

During the game, Woody keeps coming back to the bench after his shifts, complaining that his linemates won't pass to him.

"If you give, you'll get," I tell him. He's not passing today, and they aren't passing to him. That's unusual because lately they have been passing well. "Maybe I'll have you play goal," I tell him after he keeps complaining.

"Hey, at least I'd get to touch the puck."

"Hey, Mr. Arnold, how come your wife never comes to the games?" asks Coppo as the action passes our bench.

"She had enough of it when our son was growing up."

"Oh yeah, she probably dumped you," he laughs.

"No, in fact we have a big date tonight."

"Hey," he yells to the rest of the team, "Mr. Arnold's got a date with his wife tonight."

We win 8–0. Who needs those "superstars" coaching? The defence moved to forward, the forwards moved to defence. I moved two kids to forward hoping to get them their first goals. Instead, Batman, back on defence, got two goals. Swifto missed the game for medical tests. His parents have noticed he has quick heartbeats when he exerts himself. We're hoping he's okay.

The shutout means I owe the team a pizza. For every shutout I promised a pizza, so that's three so far.

Gloves is the last one out of the dressing room. I come back to see what's taking him so long. He's lifting his hockey bag over his shoulder when the weight flips him. The bag pulls him right over and onto the floor. He looks up at me. We both start roaring.

On the way home Ghost has this to say: "Did you see me that one time, when I couldn't get back too fast?" I tell him I did remember that. "That's because Fred was on my shoulders. He was falling off, and I had to stop to pick him up, a good thing I did or he might still be there." Right, Ghost. He has the whole team laughing about it.

Tomorrow we play Whitby at home. That's good – these bus trips can wear you down.

—ᴍ—

Steve and Greg are back, and so is Ghost's imaginary friend from yesterday – he's now "glued" to his shoulders. The whole team is talking about him. I think Fred's our mascot.

Swifto is back today, too, but only to watch the game with Whitby. Taped to his chest is a device to monitor his heart for irregular heartbeats. "I'll be your stick boy," he offers.

We ask the team to give and tell them they may get. In other words, if you want the other guy to pass the puck to you, you better pass it to him (or her).

Whitby takes the lead. If it wasn't for Gloves, they would have a bigger lead. Our players are flat. However, as Greg says, we are a third-period team. We're down 4–2 in the third and come back to win 5–4. Batman gets three goals.

Whitby coach Nowak is a yeller today. He yells directions to all the players. Ferrari made about four dekes to get to the goalie on one play. Although he didn't score, seeing the kid stickhandle was worth it; even his father didn't know he had it in him. Batman's three beauties today made it six goals in two games. When he scores, they are usually highlight-reel goals.

This must be a big game – Steve's wife, Rose, is here; so are his daughter and his father. Bailey is getting to be our number-one fan. My wife, Lorna, said she might even drop in. Coppo would have liked that. But she didn't. "You don't have a wife," he says.

Greg tells me about one of our parents. We heard him yelling directions at the kids during the game. It's a father who constantly criticizes our coaching behind our backs, but soft-pedals in front of us. Steve asks me if I'm going to do anything about it.

"No, he's been doing it all year and has to live with himself. As long as we're happy with our coaching, why should I get into it with him?" Steve agrees, but Greg isn't sure if we shouldn't confront him. But hockey is a hot-blooded game and we often say things during a game that many of us wish we hadn't. As long as coaches don't take the parents' attitude out on the kid, we're okay with the armchair critics.

Although we had a good comeback in the game, there was a real downer after it. While I waited for our team to vacate the dressing room, a father and his little son from the Whitby team were walking down the hallway. The father was telling the boy: "It's your fault we lost that game." I felt so sorry for the kid. Why would that kid think hockey was fun?

—⚞—

This isn't my day. Just before practice is to officially start, I'm skating backwards, calling everyone to the boards. For some reason, Swifto is lying flat on the ice. I trip over him, landing on him. I land on my elbow, a stinger, but the big concern is for Jeffrey. His heart tests were good, but can the kid survive the impact of a 190-pound man falling on him? He's laughing. Relieved, I respond with laughter too.

Many of the parents are watching from the warm room. I have to pretend that I feel no pain, but my elbow is sending shooters down my arm and freezing my hand. It's the first time I've fallen on the ice in years.

We're doing three-on-twos today, something we haven't tried before. We want to give the kids some idea of spreading out so not all of them are going after the puck. The drills are confusing for them, but necessary. We are also doing horseshoes, and I'm at centre ice when Missile ploughs into me from behind. Boom!

"Fu . . . what are you doing?" I say as I bite my tongue on the four-letter word. Missile gives me a grin and asks, "Are you all right?" Sure kid, just landed on that same elbow again. A throbbing elbow, but again you play the role and pretend there is no pain.

More practice problems. Gloves is late and in his street clothes. He tells me shyly how he forgot his equipment outside the van. Okay, he'll go out to the parking lot and get it. No problem. I think it's strange he's telling me this, it should only take a minute to go get it. Thirty minutes later there's no sign of him. He left it outside the van on his driveway *at home*!

Steve has returned from Newfoundland today after going there yesterday in his role as a representative with the NHLPA, which was donating a Zamboni and six sets of goalie equipment and sweaters to a place near Deer Lake. It's a little town of 1,600 whose people were thrilled by the gift. Steve in turn was thrilled by their hospitality, moose meat, and music.

Greg is in Florida. I'm at home icing my elbow.

— ⟶

My elbow is bruised and swollen, and my back is hurting. Who said minor novice is a non-contact sport? Steve is in Buffalo for the NHLPA. Greg is in Florida for the CBC. Bill and I are at the Kinsmen arena for the minor novice Petes.

"Will that affect my ice time?" asks Missile, referring to the centre-ice collision from the last practice.

"Only if *you're* hurt," I assure him.

Running a practice with only two people is not a good idea. We can't keep our eyes on enough kids. The kids haven't been listening lately so I've made two new rules.

1. Players have to ask to get a drink of water.
2. If one player is messing around while the coaches are talking, the entire team will skate around the ice.

It doesn't take long for one player to start messing around, so the whole team is made to go around the ice. The practice goes well after that.

Ann Millen is back from Florida where she says it rained and was very cold. Great! Lorna and I are to leave for Fort Myers Beach, Florida, on Monday for five days. Greg, Steve, and Bill will be at Tuesday's practice; I have power skating scheduled for Thursday.

I hate to leave them . . . but Florida beckons. It can't be colder there than here. I'd rather walk barefoot in cold Florida sand than in the three feet of white stuff we have at home.

But first we have a game to play – on Super Bowl Sunday.

—⁂—

This is the NFL's Super Bowl Sunday so before the game starts against the Central Wolves, I ask the kids what they can do on the ice today that starts with the letter *S*.

"Skate! Shoot! Save!" they yell.

I remind them about the pizza for a shutout. Bill and Steve groan, believing this promise will put a jinx on the team. Old wives' tales! The team needs to think about team goals. A shutout is a team goal. Just like eating pizza.

We talk about some other S-words such as "short shifts" and "staying out of the sin bin." Then we're ready for the game.

Today is another joy to watch. The kids are backchecking, taking short shifts, and we block four shots, which is four more than we have all year. They are looking for the shutout.

Woody is on fire. He's all over the place, checking, carrying the puck, passing, and it pays off with three goals and an assist. We have a 4–0 lead when Central "scores." It's obvious to all, including one of the referees, that the puck hit the post, but the goal will stand. We don't protest.

We have a lot of injuries today. Steve isn't impressed with the tactics employed by the other team and their constant slashing. Our kids are coming back to the bench with slashed wrists. Some of the ones who never cry are crying today. As they come back to the bench to Johnny's care, I get out my cellphone and offer to telephone their doctor. They laugh and the injuries are gone.

We win 5–1 (maybe I did jinx the shutout). After the game I tell the team I owe them another pizza. As far as we're concerned it's a shutout. Bill hands out cupcakes, Johnny hands out his traditional candy.

In the morning, Lorna and I will be on our way to Florida. Steve and Greg are off to Denver Thursday for the NHL All-Star game festivities. That's why I booked a power-skating coach for Thursday.

—ⁿⁿ—

We're in beautiful Fort Myers Beach, Florida. My son calls to tell me the power-skating coach has cancelled out of Thursday. Great. Bill will have to scramble for a practice. I tell my son to go to today's practice, let Steve know, so Bill can get the pucks and cones I left and, with a bit of luck, get some help for Thursday.

I head back to the sandy white beach and the eighty-one-degree (Fahrenheit) temperature, with wife, book, lunch, sunscreen, and cold ones.

"Oh yeah, Scott," I tell my son. "Tell Steve and Bill I'm really missing the snow and cold and I'll have one for them on the beach."

I've arranged to be back Friday night so I won't miss any games.

8

It's Not About Hockey, It's About Kids

Back home in Peterborough a freezing-rain warning was announced. I wonder why we live here . . . it must be the hockey.

I haven't been in the house thirty minutes when the president of the minor Petes council is on the telephone, reminding me about playoffs, ice scheduling, and parental door duties after our regular season finishes at the end of the month.

A couple of days later, at the rink, Woody calls out to me in the dressing room. "Hey, Mr. Arnold, didn't you get the job?"

"What job?"

"Assistant coach of Tampa Bay," he replies in all seriousness. Several other players ask the same thing. What's going on here?

We played Whitby today. Before the game I ask the defence what the forward options are, and the forwards the defence options. Goalies? Everyone should know that: They have to stop the puck.

It was a good game. Whitby has really improved. They out-played us, but our goalies did what they got paid the big bucks to do; they were awesome.

Whitby coach Nowak hasn't changed much at all. He was constantly yelling directions at his players, and at the referees. He argued about offside calls and faceoff calls, but none of his yelling changed a thing.

Officiating minor hockey is a tough job. I got suspended two years ago in a minor novice game when the referee said I had jumped into the other team's bench. It was actually the other team's coach who jumped into *our* bench after I questioned his overplaying of one of his stars while they were beating us 10–0. The ref didn't see it that way. The other team's coach did, though, and phoned me at home that night to apologize. The refs make only between fifteen and twenty-five dollars per night. They have all been to clinics, but like everyone else, they are still learning. Some officiating in minor hockey is absolutely atrocious, but most of it is good, fair, and impartial.

Gary Baldwin has been a minor-hockey referee for several years and organizes the officials in Peterborough. He's also a public school teacher who's a former captain of the local provincial junior A team and a former coach of the Peterborough midget AAA team. Gary refereed many of our games this year. His referees say they enjoyed doing our games because we never yelled at them and our parents rarely did. When he had first heard Steve and Greg were helping coach, he thought, "Isn't it neat to have two former NHL players willing to give something back to the game by helping coach the youngest AAA team in our system.

"Then I thought that this was nothing special since thousands of volunteers do the same volunteering each year on thousands of minor hockey teams throughout the province. Nonetheless, the presence of NHL players certainly enhances the credibility of the coaching staff for the system, the parents, and the players.

"What I saw as a referee [at our games] from the start of the season through to the end was a real sense that the kids were enjoying themselves. Their skill development improved drastically, especially their skating ability. They also seemed to have a very good sense of positional play, yet when I mentioned this to Steve Larmer one day he told me that very little time was spent on positional play. The kids simply moved to a spot on the ice where the opponents weren't, to receive a pass – a very simple concept, yet so few teams understand this. As a referee my dialogue with most coaches, I believe, is cordial, yet there was always a sense that with the minor novice Petes team there was a general enjoyment and satisfaction by the coaching staff by watching their players perform.

"From the bench the coaching staff was very encouraging of the players when they returned to the bench. The coaches were all at eye level with the players and did not stand on the top of the benches like so many coaches do. They seemed to make a concerted effort to get down at the level of the players. Constant feedback to the players was evident.

"The reaction of parents was also different. The parents were noticeably more quiet, almost reserved. On only a few occasions did I hear any criticism of the officials. I heard no shouting or coaching from the stands, although there were the usual oohs and aahs when a goal was scored or a big save was made. The impression I had was that the parents bought into the philosophy of encouragement and being positive rather than one of shouting and coaching from the stands, a marked contrast to many other rinks in which minor Petes teams and others play.

"The other thing that struck me was that the kids genuinely seemed to enjoy playing the game. Everyone played, and no power-play or penalty-kill teams were evident. There were very few penalties called in most of the games, but to be fair, in most minor novice games fewer penalties are the norm. As an official, I did enjoy officiating this team."

—∿∿—

We win a 2–1 thriller against Whitby. After the game I tell the kids, "Sometimes the goalies win a game for you. This was one of those games." We give them a big round of applause. Charlie and Mitch eat it up.

—∿∿—

We have the full complement of coaches. Today at practice, Steve has them working on three-on-ohs, two-on-ohs, five-on-ohs. He's impressed with a column written by Ken Dryden, the former NHL goalie who is now president of the Toronto Maple Leafs. "Ed, you've been right on. He's saying what we are doing," reports Steve. Hey, Steve's doing it. I'm just following, but you know what? That makes me feel very good.

The team skates another disciplinary lap today. They also listen better today. The CBC has sent *Hockey Night in Canada* and CBC Sports hats to the team. The kids love the hats. It was a thoughtful gesture on the part of producer Paul Harrington. I wish he could have seen their faces.

Steve's young nephew is playing in the church-league game after our practice. Church league is a house league, but when those kids are on the ice playing the game, they are stars as well.

"Maybe that's where we should coach next year, far less commitment," I say to Steve offhandedly.

"You know, I was thinking about that."

Neither of us knows what we're doing next year. Coaching is fun, but it is a major time commitment, one which our employers and family have allowed us to continue with.

Greg tells us he thinks the kids might be getting burned out. We don't agree. As we watch them at practice laughing and screaming with delight, we still don't see signs of burnout.

"Maybe if you were around a bit more you wouldn't think these things," says Steve. He's teasing, of course.

"Good point," says Greg. "They also don't like the power skating," he adds.

"Sometimes it's not always what we like that is good for us," I respond.

"Good point," says Greg. Poor Loops, he really cares about minor hockey, but he's just not here enough. When he is here, he's an excellent coach. He gets involved and makes some great contributions on the ice.

"Oh, by the way," Steve tells him, "if you're going to tell everyone on national TV that you're coaching with me, try to show up a bit more often." We laugh at this one. Greg had mentioned his involvement with the minor Petes during a hockey broadcast on Saturday. (A friend of mine heard the comment and was going to phone Greg and ask him, "I thought you guys were coaching with Ed Arnold?")

"Aren't you guys full of vinegar today?" says Greg, laughing. Actually, we probably had more fun than the kids. Is that a bad thing?

—⁓—

A major snowstorm, the biggest of the season, means only half the team shows for practice. Bartman is the first there.

"You're not cancelling practice, are you?" he asks as I enter the rink.

"Nope. Even if it's just you and me, we'll have a practice." For the second time this year I arrive before Steve at a practice. He gets there about ten minutes later. He has a good excuse, though – he was shovelling his parents' driveway.

"You bring your workboots, Bart?" he asks little Kirk, who says he's got his snow boots.

"No, your workboots, your skates," says Steve.

It's amazing that *anyone* showed up, but nine players do, and for those who did it was a treat. For the first half-hour Steve and I take on whoever arrives, in a game of pond hockey. Okay, I exaggerate, Steve takes them on and I feed him the puck (isn't that what Denis Savard always did?).

Timbit and Coppo join our team. It's us against the other seven players. Timbit gets seven goals.

"Not many kids can say they got seven goals assisted by Larmer and Arnold," I say to him. He flashes one of the biggest smiles you'd ever see.

It is a half-hour of joyous fun. Woody goes down after receiving one of my elbows, then decides to "shadow" me for the rest of the game.

"I've almost had it – this is hard work," I tell Steve, who not only knows what I'm talking about, but agrees. Try chasing nine kids around for a half-hour some day.

This is how Steve grew up, playing shinny in his backyard rink and the schoolyard rink until the moon came up or parents started blinking the porch lights off and on as a signal for the kids to come home. He would skate before and after school. He'd be on the rink all day Saturday and Sunday, coming home only for lunch. Even then he wouldn't take off his skates. He'd kneel, pushing the food down so he could rush back to play some more. He seldom got cold. Sometimes they were so warm, they would have to take their jackets off.

Bill joins us in the middle of practice, and we do some shooting, skating, and passing drills, then set up a scrimmage with a tennis ball.

Steve and I talked before practice again about what we're going to do next year. Some parents have been asking us and we're still not sure. Steve won't be back as a coach. He knows his workload is going to be heavier next year, and he wants to free up his weekends. I'm not quite sure what I'll do. Steve loves practice and wouldn't mind being a practice coach who doesn't have to go to the games. Our hearts aren't in coming back and cutting any of these great kids at tryout time. We both love coaching the kids. It's a chance to forget life for an hour or so. You can relive the joys of childhood and lose yourself. The fun is in the freedom, seeing these kids enjoying the same thing and watching them improve. Oh, well, we'll worry about the future later.

I've written a letter for the parents and Steve has approved it. I know what can happen when the playoffs approach, and I don't want parents to get any wrong ideas. We're in first place. Steve and I don't care about this, but we know the players and parents have been continuing to go on the Internet to find out the statistics. The success of this team does not, and never has, depended on winning. It hinges on whether they still enjoy coming to practice (they all enjoy games) and whether they are improving and being treated fairly.

Here's the letter we will send to the parents:

This is a note for the parents as the regular season winds down and the playoffs come before us. Hockey is Canada's game and it is an emotional one. Playoffs make it more emotional and exciting.

We just wanted to let parents know that while playoffs bring on new importance, it won't mean a change in our philosophy.

We think the kids have come a long way, we think they are a real team. We also believe we have been fair. They have all experienced power plays, short-handed situations, first-minute and last-minute situations. This will continue in the playoffs.

The next line up will be the next line out in any situation. There will be no double-shifting. We may look at changing positions or linemates as we do in other games, but nothing unusual.

We would like the kids to go as far as possible because they deserve it, but we won't be shortening the bench or using a win-at-all-costs tactic to accomplish this. It will be up to the kids.

You're all paying and they're all playing!

We hope you'll agree with this and wish all the kids well in the coming weeks.

Another bus trip, this time to Oshawa. The bus leaves at 3:15 p.m. for the 5:00 p.m. game. Little Stevie Larmer, it turns out, has been up to some tricks. It was he who told the kids I was in Tampa Bay applying for an assistant coaching job with the Lightning. Bill and John were taking the rap, but the kids and parents informed me today who the culprit was. We didn't know how widespread his story had become. Woody couldn't get to sleep. Swifto searched for news from Tampa by way of the satellite dish. Even some parents thought I was applying for a job in Tampa. By the time the rest of the community hears about it, the story will have taken a life of its own. Now I know why so many people were asking if I got the job. It's a good story . . . and I owe him one.

"It shows you how much they care about you, though," says Steve.

I told the team I turned the Tampa job down because I wanted to stay with a winner.

The Oshawa team has come a long way. We had to depend on our goalies again to pull out a 3–1 win. The Oshawa coach had more Larmer hockey cards with him for autographing. I wonder again if the other coaches prepare more carefully for games against us because we have Steve and Greg. I don't know, but there may be a tendency to play the better players more often than the others and use defensive systems against us. There may be more coaching to win than instructing (just developing the players) when we play. Greg and Steve agree.

Today's game is a rough one. Oshawa plays with physical contact. We had the worst officiating I've seen this year. One referee came over on three separate occasions to apologize for blowing calls.

"I almost said something today," Steve tells me after the game. For him to be that upset you know there were problems. It's a good thing Loops Millen wasn't there (he was in Vancouver). I'm not sure he could have controlled his anger – not at the refs, but at the physical style of play. However, we took most of the penalties and they were usually after the whistle. I talked to the team about this later. The positive side of things is that we killed off three five-on-threes and eight penalties, and used everyone to do it. The other positive thing is that of all the games we've played, we've only had one really bad game by refs – that's excellent in any hockey. I bet the refs can't say that about coaches or parents.

Mitch stops three pucks with his face mask. "That's usin' your head, Mitch," Bill tells his son after the game. Gloves stops a breakaway. Coppo is very impressive today, as are Timbit and Hicksie. They are making excellent decisions about when to carry the puck, when to pass, and when to hang on to it. They are showing real patience. Ghost blocks three shots from the point today. Gloves asks, after the third blocked shot, "How can he block the shots, if he's a ghost?"

"They can't see him," I reply.

Gloves has a new trapper today. "Does it have a hole in it like your dad's did?" asks Steve.

I jokingly assess "fines" against the players who missed practice Thursday. I didn't expect them to make it because of the storm, but tell them they must pay the coach a bubblegum. Ferrari paid me with a muffin.

"I have gum right now," Nicole told me before the game "but you're not getting it." She later gave me a single piece of gum.

The bus trip home is another of the noisier ones. We have pizza, doughnuts, chips, and Gatorade. I usually turn the food down and do so again tonight. I never know if Lorna and I will be having supper when I get home (turns out it was a wise decision tonight because we did have supper). The bus is messy when we pull into the parking lot so I tell the kids they aren't getting off until the bus is clean.

"I have to get off," says Mitch with a pained looked on his face.

"Nope, the whole team has to clean up."

"But I have to go to the bathroom," he says, clamping his legs and running to the rink as I open the door to let him out.

"I have to go too," says Gloves with a big grin. Good try, Glovesy.

If the coach of a kids' team was asked if he's going to coach next year after a Saturday-night bus trip, the answer would probably be no.

Meanwhile, I have a chance to pay Steve back for the Tampa joke. When we arrive in Peterborough, he can't unlock his truck door. It's malfunctioning or frozen. Should I leave him in the parking lot?

"Well, friend?" he asks, looking at me as I warm the car engine. All right, get in. I still owe him.

—ᚁ—

Practice. "A hockey team is only successful as a team if it plays as a team. Individuals will not make a team successful. I think Saturday's game was one of the worst we've played as a team, because we had too many players being individuals. It is more fun being a team – that's the fun of hockey," Steve tells the team before practice. It's the first time he has addressed them like this and they are listening. He tells them they weren't passing, skating, shooting, and thinking as a team. "You weren't making good decisions."

I think his words help us through a particularly difficult drill, one we felt wasn't going to work, but came out perfectly. It starts as a five-on-two, then develops back up the ice as a two-on-one, and then a one-on-one. The kids are excellent.

The sixty to seventy pucks we usually have in our old milk crate are now only twenty to thirty pucks. "If you check the kids' bags you might find some more," says Bill.

Greg is at practice tonight, but has to go home. He forgot his skates. Poor Loops. He'll leave practice a bit early . . . he has to be in five cities in six days for hockey broadcasts. His life only sounds glamorous.

The coaches got some chocolate hearts today for valentines. Ghost gives me mine.

"Thanks, Ghost, I really appreciate it," I tell him.

"I didn't give them to you. Katherine [our manager] told me to," he says. Okay.

"I have two ice ponds in front of my house," says Nicole "Jets" Gifford proudly.

"Do you put the cows on the ice?"

"No, cows aren't allowed on the ice," she replies. It's clear from the scorn in her voice she's thinking, "What are you, an idiot?"

"How about cow patties?"

"We play with them sometimes." Jets is her new nickname because of her speed. We now have a missile, a rocket, and some jets playing for us.

Then there is Ferrari. "I got suspended [from school] for one day today for hitting another kid," he says sadly. His dad tells me about his suspension as well.

I tell him the team must also discipline him. Jonathan doesn't expect this. "I'll suspend you for seven weeks in April," I say. Jonathan smiles. He knows the season is over before that. When we were young we used to get the strap for such things, or detentions, or extra reading – now the schools send the kids home . . . that's punishment?

It seems there are changes and desire for change everywhere. Steve informs me he's going to Davis Inlet for a week for the NHLPA. (This may be my chance to get him back . . . Mr. Larmer has taken a job as a sled operator in the north.) Swifto left for Florida more than a week ago. We still don't have him back. Coppo wants to play in a native tournament in Sudbury during the March break. It may be held at the same time as our playoffs. He's important to us, and those native games are important to him. Wheelsie is now wearing a Toronto Maple Leafs hat. He's no longer a Canadiens fan. "The Canadiens are Americans now," he shouts to me. The Habs were purchased by an American two weeks ago. Ghost asks today if he can play forward the next game. I say we'll see, but tell him I really like him on defence and he's important to us at that position. He shrugs and says, "Okay."

—m—

It was the first time Steve, Bill, and I had frozen toes after the practice – it's that cold. Not as cold as it is on the twenty outdoor rinks that volunteers in Peterborough look after, but cold enough.

Swifto returned from Florida today after visiting Disneyland. Ghost's dad has heard that his son asked to play forward and assures me it wasn't the father's suggestion. No problem, it's minor novice and I'll try to get him up front again.

A parent has given us the league standings. We are two points ahead of the second-place team with two games left. Those games are both against the second-place team, Clarington, which has three games left. Our fate is in our hands.

Who would have thought it? "And we just let them do their thing, it's amazing," says Steve. The coaches aren't going to get too hyped about the playoff situation, but we don't think it's wrong for the kids. The pursuit of winning can make hockey fun. We'll make sure it remains fun, win or lose, but we aren't going to take away the competitiveness.

I told some kids during one drill today that if they scored in practice they'd get a bubble gum at the next game. If they missed, they'd owe me one. I owe Wheelsie four gums, Woody one, Batman one, and some of them owe me some. What can I say? It helps pass the time and they work harder. Besides, we all like gum.

Coppo's mum brings me a program about the native tournament. It is a big deal, and we don't want Wesley to miss it, even though it may affect our prospects. I telephone his family after practice to tell them I'd prefer that they go to the tournament.

It has special meaning to them and I believe it's important that Wesley not miss it. They tell me they are committed to our team and will travel back and forth, but I don't want them to be concerned about that. Besides, Swifto just got back from Florida. I went to Florida. Steve is going to Florida. Greg misses quite a bit. Bill went to basketball and hockey games. Johnny misses games. (A fine set of examples we are.) Minor novice hockey shouldn't be the top priority in a kid's life, especially when it comes to their heritage, culture, and traditions.

The team doesn't seem cohesive on the ice today. Steve calls it sloppy. Rocket shows up, only to tell me he has sprained his ankle at school and will miss practice.

"I hurt it at gym, coach," he tells me.

"Jim who? You were probably chasing your valentine around for a kiss," I tell him. This kid's smile is awesome. His dad is there to help Riley explain. I'm not sure I help Lloyd by saying, "The best thing for a sprained ankle is McDonald's, milkshakes, ice cream, and television."

—◊—

Away game. Our bus arrives about ten minutes late and it's *cold*. We're off to Darlington, about a thirty-five-minute drive. Bailey Larmer, Steve's daughter, is on the bus today. I tell her if we win she owes me some Reese's Pieces.

I pay off my bubble-gum debts to the players from Thursday's practice (I end up giving everyone a piece, of course). Steve has a head cold and gravelly voice. Bill is fine. Johnny's with the Petes today but came to see us off and left a bag of licorice. Greg is in Edmonton with the CBC. Rocket's "sprained" ankle is okay.

"Ed, Ferrari won't be at the game today, he's sick," Jonathan's mum tells me on the telephone. (The parents continue to use the nicknames.)

The team is relaxed. I tell them a team is like the bus we just drove on. If all the parts aren't working, it's not going to get us to our destination. Timbit will move from defence to forward for Ferrari. I'm trying to get him a goal. He and C. P., another defenceman, are the only two without goals so far. They do so many other things so well on defence. They've had their chances to score but can't "bury the biscuit."

Steve also talks to the players about playing as a team. Then he whispers to Nathan, "I've got a feeling about you today." Larse gives his freckled-face spacey-toothed smile. Gloves pretends he's snoring as we talk. They've heard it all before.

I briefly underscore to Bill and Steve that we have to stick with playing the kids, there'll be no changes in philosophy. "Maybe we should call up someone from our farm team," says Steve, as a joke, reminding us all not to get too serious.

It's only seven seconds into the game. Timbit takes a shot on net and scores. His first goal. Words can't describe the expression on his face. His teammates are as happy for him as they are for the goal. We save the puck for him.

It's a back-and-forth game. Into the second period it's 4–4. Our team is grinding today. They are playing as a team and controlling the play. We continue complimenting the players for their good plays when they come off the ice. They're knocking the puck off the boards during this game to get past defenders. That's something we practised last week.

Wheelsie is turning into quite a playmaker. We start to take the lead. In the third period I move C. P. to forward to replace Timbit. On his first shift, Missile has a breakaway with C. P. He moves the puck over to him and C. P. scores his first one. I don't know what makes us happier, that pass or that goal, but C. P.'s face and the hug they give each other say it all.

Batman takes a cross-check to the stomach and comes off the ice crying. Never mind – he scores a goal on both of his next two shifts. (He loves to score when he's hurting.) Some days things just go well. Hicksie has really caught on to defence. He not only knows when to hustle for the puck, but when to go with it and pass. Jeff Braithwaite knows how to direct the opposition into the boards. I compliment him on an excellent defensive play.

"That was excellent, Jeff."

"It's Ghost," he reminds me.

Coppo skates as hard going up the ice as he does coming back. It inspires the checking game. We win 10–4. Nine players have scored. As we come off the ice, Bailey Larmer is in the hallway, handing me my Reese's Pieces.

We tell the team how proud we are of their passing plays and teamwork then hand out Johnny's licorice. I also give C. P. his first-goal-scoring puck. "How about Bake's?" he asks, not knowing I had already given Timbit his, but that's how thoughtful these kids are.

Winning is fun, but it always makes for louder bus trips home. We'll be home by 5:30 p.m. but not before we've seen Gummies go up noses; Gatorades mixed with sodas; and licorice dropped in Gatorades. We've heard burps, screaming, whistling, and laughter. We've also smelled what mum and dad used to smell in the diapers.

When I get home, I look at the score sheet and see that every player, except the goalies, got a point in today's game. That's something I'll point out at Tuesday's practice.

As we're about to get off the bus I look around at Timbit and C. P. They're still revelling in their success. Steve, catching my eye, says, "You've created a monster." We know they'll probably want to be forwards again. Oh well, it is only minor novice; it is only a hockey game.

—⁓—

The thing I dislike most about practices is going to the locker room at the newspaper where I work, changing from my suit into my sweats, putting my work clothes on hangers, loading them into the car, rushing to the rink, getting out the bucket of pucks, cones, sticks, and the rest of the gear. Rush, rush, rush.

The thing I like most about practices is watching the kids step onto the ice and enjoying that freedom. Greg had said the same thing to me today about why he loves coming to these practices. He probably didn't like today's practice: we made him skate a lap because he was late. He did it in fun and the kids loved it.

What else don't I like about coaching these kids? The colds I get. I have another one. Ghost isn't here today, he has the flu. J. G. may be really sick. His parents are taking him to the hospital tomorrow to see what blood tests reveal. He could have what is called Kawasaki's disease, a heart infection, which would put him in the hospital. It reminds you again why hockey isn't really that important in the total picture.

Today is testing day. We're comparing what the kids did in September and December to what they can do now to gauge if the players have improved as individuals and as a team. We also have a game using a tennis ball.

The Coppaways brought me some fresh fish today. "That's bribery," says Greg. I'll take it. The little story about me applying for a coaching job in Tampa has got into the local newspaper. I tell the parents and coaches I will pay them back, eventually. Wheelsie is at a lodge all week skiing and sledding.

Dave Carter, a parent from the kids' team that plays after our practices, paid us a great compliment today. He's been watching our practices and thinks they are the most organized he has seen. "You guys don't waste any ice, or any time, and you're so well-organized. That's the way it should be when ice costs so much [about $110 for fifty minutes in Peterborough]," he says.

It's not that hard. The Canadian Hockey Association coaching booklets contain all kinds of practice tips. You don't have to have played in the NHL to implement them. Some of them appear to be more confusing than they really are, but the basics are there.

It's 6:00 p.m. I left the house at 6:50 a.m. I'll phone Ghost and J. G. tonight to see how they are, have some supper, watch some television, and go to the wake of an old friend.

Indeed, some things are worth coaching for . . . and one of those things is a big feed of fresh pickerel. Lorna and I ate Wesley's family's fish last night . . . talk about melting in your mouth and tantalizing your taste buds. I write Coppo a note to give him at the next practice. "What a great supper my wife and I had last night; fries and fresh pickerel! Whew! I had to cook it up, and that was probably the only problem with it, but it tasted great. Not only was it great fish, but it was all cleaned and ready to cook for me. (You probably did that, right?) My wife and I really appreciated it. It took us only a few minutes to gobble it down. Now I can coach on a full stomach . . . although it's big enough now. Thanks again."

There are some things not worth coaching for . . . Steve had $150 stolen from his pants. He left them in the dressing room. We leave our room unlocked while we're on the ice so it was our own fault. J. G. is still sick and is now in the hospital. Poor kid.

Practice is lively, the kids have a jump to them and as always have a lot of fun. Ghost is back. He's always worth a few laughs.

Today he does some figure-skating moves. He lost his gloves. Rocket has left his stick at home. Sure, they're ready.

I'm thinking of changing M. G.'s (Mitch Gillam's) name to Thrill. The saves he makes are so thrilling. Today he stopped one off his helmet. He likes the name change.

Steve is off to Montreal tomorrow for Canadian Hockey Association meetings. He'll be back for the middle of Sunday's game – we hope. The parents are buzzing about tomorrow night's televising of the CBC special. They're also buzzing about Sunday's last regular-season game that will decide first place. Oh, oh.

—ɷ—

The CBC show was excellent. They titled it "The Meaning." Steve did a great job in his interview, as did the kids.

In the interview, Steve said coaching minor-league hockey was the last thing he thought he would be doing but "you know, somebody made minor hockey a very good experience for me and it's nice to be able to give that back." My favourite quote from Steve was one we had repeated often: "Nobody wants to be yelled at. That just tightens the kid right up, and they're gonna go out there and play scared to make a mistake and they're gonna stand around and not get involved. We don't care if kids make mistakes. We want them to skate, and if it doesn't work this time it might work the next time, but keep that attitude of I can, I can.

"The problem with yelling at a child from the bench is little Johnny is skating down the ice and you're yelling pass it and Mum's yelling 'shoot it' and Dad's yelling 'dump it' and they've got to stop and think 'okay, what do I do? Mum's telling me to shoot it, Dad's telling me to pass, coach is telling me to dump it, hmmm.' Well, guess what? Somebody's taken the puck off you and gone the other way."

Jets stole the show when she said, "Well, I like to skate. I like to shoot and score, and I like to be tough in hockey. Well, I don't think they [her teammates], like, think I'm a girl because, like, I don't think they'll treat me bad because I'm a teammate. Because they're tough I can be tough too."

The ending broke us all up. Ferrari is sitting on the bench beside Steve while the game is in progress. Ferrari has no idea his words are being taped or the camera across the ice is focused on him. He looks up at Steve, smiles, and says, "Time sure flies when you're having fun."

Greg calls from Calgary: "Hey, Hollywood," he says, wanting to know what I thought of the show. I thought Greg's participation with the team could have been mentioned, but he says that as a CBC employee he didn't think it was appropriate, that it could be seen as self-serving. My mother, who lives in Fredericton, New Brunswick, called after watching the show and put it in perspective. "It looks like you've put on a few pounds," she says.

Today is the game against Clarington to decide who takes first place. Steve thinks our game is scrambly play. I think we aren't playing as a team. And Greg wonders if the kids are agitated because the game is for first place. We agree things may get worse in the playoffs.

Greg is not happy the other team shortens its bench today, and he's not happy they yell at the referees. It doesn't seem to bother him that we lose 4–1. Maybe we came up so flat because we've been hit with illnesses. Timbit had the flu. Missile had a cold. M. G. had pneumonia. Two others were sick. J. G. is still sick so we moved different defencemen to the wing during each period. Three of them got to play forward. We did look like individuals on the ice. Oh well, we ended the season tied for first. Nothing wrong with that. Our record was eighteen wins, ten losses, and two ties. Not bad at all.

We will play Whitby in the playoffs.

"Hey, Mr. Arnold, how did the Habs do last night?" ask a couple of the kids, who know they lost to the Leafs 5–1. "We could beat that team," yells Coppo.

I agree. But maybe not today.

I finished analyzing the team evaluations and have put the results together. The team average has improved in all areas. I added a chart to the report to show their times in the drills they did at their first practice September 5. That set the benchmark. We had timed them again on December 5 with the same drills, then again on February 20. Each time the team showed major improvements.

Team Averages

Up and back power skate with puck

Sept. 5	15.11 seconds
Dec. 5	14.58
Feb. 20	13.80

Six cone puck drill

Sept. 5	18.74 seconds
Dec. 5	17.75
Feb. 20	15.40

Crossover full ice

Sept. 5	23.52 seconds
Dec. 5	21.80
Feb. 20	21.00

Cone and back

Sept. 5	27.7 seconds
Dec. 5	20.5
Feb. 20	19.0

When we met with them individually, we asked the parents if they had any complaints, problems, or concerns. None of them said they did.

Over the course of the season, we scored 138 goals and allowed only 85 goals against. In the entire Eastern Ontario AAA league, our team was tied for second. We scored the third-most goals in the league and tied for allowing the fewest goals against. The only team with a better record in the entire league was Markham, which won 28, lost only 1, tied 1, scored 159 goals, and allowed 85 goals against. We had played every one of our seventeen kids in every shift of every game in every situation.

Practice time. Greg wants to have a controlled scrimmage. Although we set it up, he can tell I'm not too excited about it. We're stopping play, positioning players, and telling them what to do. I suggest to Greg that we should be telling them this is an option they have, but it is up to them to make the right decisions for the team. He agrees and brings the team together to tell them the drills are only options, not must-do things.

Greg is concerned the parents might be putting pressure on the kids because of the playoffs and wants to issue them a letter.

I tell him to go ahead but later he changes his mind. The letter he wrote but didn't send expressed our appreciation for the way the players' parents had stood by us all year. He also pointed out, however, that the kids would be putting pressure on themselves with the playoffs coming up and the parents should continue to praise their kids but be careful not to add to the stress.

—◊—

Woody gets a new nickname today . . . Superman. His father washed his blue practice jersey and parts of it got bleached. The other kids are asking about it so I tell them it was caused by his speed on the ice. He moves so fast that the blue got blurred just like Superman.

Nathan gets a new nickname, too: Trigger, because he pulled the trigger on his big shot Sunday. I've been watching him all year. Every practice he gets more focused. When one line is doing a drill, he'll practise puck-handling skills on his own while the other kids just talk and wait for their turn.

Rocket has the flu today, but J. G. is back as healthy as ever. Thank goodness. That was a big scare for both the family and the kid. As he steps on the ice he looks at me, smiles, pushes off on his skates, and says, "I feel great."

We have our first pushing match at practice. Two teammates almost battle it out. They won't stop. I have to break it up with a sharp whistle. I talk with the team about being teammates and tell them I don't want to see it again. It takes about ten seconds before one kid pushes another! They are just horsing around to get my goat. All I can do is laugh.

"Hey, Mr. Arnold, when do the playoffs start?" several of them ask. We don't know yet, but soon. As we leave the rink: "We'll see you, Teak, don't forget to bring some gum to the next practice," says Glovesy.

9

MARCH

Final Period

S ome days don't go well. My daughter did a university project
on an old Apple laptop of mine. We can't transfer the data.
In other words, we can't get it out. I got a new bedroom television today. When I got it home, it was broken; I took it back,
brought another one home. Just made it to practice.

"Do you know when the playoffs start, Ed?" asks one parent.

"No, not yet, the Ontario Minor Hockey Association is
putting it together."

"Do you know when they *might* start, Ed?" No . . . and then
six other noes to six other parents. Then the kids ask, "Hey, Mr.
Arnold, when's our next game?" Don't know, but our next practice is today.

Steve is in Labrador. Greg is in Ottawa. Bill and I are at the rink. Wheelsie and Rocket aren't . . . they have a major case of the flu. Wheelsie's mum said he was feeling so sick that he said to her, "Mum, do me a favour and kill me."

Elephant-memory Gloves asks, "Hey, Teak, got any gum?"

"I'll bring it to the next game."

"When's that?" Don't know.

I finally get home today after 6:00 p.m. My telephone call display shows that my wife has called from work. She needs a ride. Great! I just brought home some hot pizza. Back out I go. By 7:00 p.m. we're settled in. The phone rings.

"Ed, we start our playoffs on Sunday at home," says Katherine. I take half the parents' list, she takes the other, and we start phoning.

Superman isn't invincible. He's sick with the flu. This could be quite an opening playoff. We're down three players for the best-of-five series.

—⚡—

The first playoff game against Whitby is in Peterborough. Wheelsie is still sick. Several others have a cold and Coppo "doesn't feel well."

We stick with our usual approach. The first period is a dandy. Gloves is great in net, as is the Whitby goalie. The period ends in a 0–0 draw. Whitby has its star player on the ice whenever it can.

The second period is much the same. However, a penalty shot is called against us. They score. Greg, Steve, Johnny, and Billy are all here for this game. "I wonder if they'll switch their goalie?" asks Greg. I don't believe they will. I've been in too many novice playoff games. I know what happens. The coaches start playing to win. The parents want to win. The odd kid gets forgotten.

Coppo heads to the dressing room and vomits. We think he's done for the game but he shows up again. For the first time this year, a discipline matter pops up on the bench. Greg has sent a player to the dressing room for head-butting one of his own teammates while on the bench. I agree with what he did, but didn't like banishing him for the entire game. He's part of the team. I send Johnny to get him back. I talk to him about the incident and he apologizes. End of story.

Whitby scores two short-handed goals. We're behind 3–0 with about six minutes left in the game. We don't give up and remain positive on the bench. We can hear parents from both teams screaming, yelling at the top of their lungs: "Skate, skate. Skate hard. Pass it. He's wide open. Shoot it in. What's wrong with you, ref? Who's paying you? Come on, check him."

Trigger scores. Two minutes later, Jets gets another after we pull the goalie with two minutes left. It's 3–2, but we can't stop their star player, who gets his third of the game. That's why they are star players.

We tell the kids they played a good game, and they should forget the loss and get back in it tomorrow night. There really isn't much else to say. Both teams played well – a couple of breaks here and there and it might have been different.

We have so many sick kids. It will be interesting tomorrow night.

—◊—

Oh, oh, we're in trouble. There is a snowstorm. Ghost forgot his stick. Trigger forgot his tie. Gloves isn't feeling well. Wheelsie is still at home sick. Missile is sick. And Loops is drawing positions on a hockey board. The old X-and-O trick.

The game isn't that interesting; we get blown out 7–3. Whitby has some skilled players – five of their goals are top-shelf. It is our worst defeat in months. Our September team showed up.

The Whitby Wildcats have war paint striped across their cheeks. I have no idea how the Coppaways feel about this, but I don't like it. Whitby also has a big parent-cheering squad. Our parents were ready. They had the noisemakers, the pompoms, and the posters of support. They just didn't have the team.

Whitby deserved the win. I don't like kids playing systems at this age, or coaches yelling at their players and the referees, but they were the better team. Whitby played their other goalie, thank goodness, and didn't shorten their bench as much as in the first game. They didn't need to.

By the third period I had moved all of our defence to forward to try to get more fun into the game. Ghost went twenty feet offside looking for one pass.

"That was the greatest offside I have ever seen," I tell him later.

"Hey, thanks, coach," he replies.

The players got over the loss in minutes, devouring pizza and being as noisy on the bus as usual. The adults worry about losses more than the kids do.

"This isn't life-and-death stuff," Steve reminds us. "We can't change things now, we've done all we can do and now we have to see what the kids are made of."

"Maybe the parents are putting too much pressure on them," suggests Greg.

"Whitby kids have parents too," I remind him.

"Don't worry, we'll beat them, Mr. Arnold," says Timbit. He says his brother's atom team won 14–1 in a playoff game Friday night. They played the same team Sunday and lost 8–7 in overtime.

—⁂—

The day after our second playoff loss, the *National Post* ran an article about minor hockey referees taking verbal abuse and how bad the situation has become. I had seen yet another example of the trend just the weekend before. I was at an out-of-town atom (eleven-year-olds) game on Saturday. The three coaches for one team were yelling and berating the refs, and they were screaming at their kids. The team had only eleven players and was shortening the bench. The other team, which played every one of their players, won 7–4.

What I had seen at that game and what I had read were very much on my mind as I prepared for evaluation interviews. When I met with the players individually, I told them how awesome they had been, how hard they had worked, how they deserved the improvement. They listened intently as I said things like "We're very proud of you. Remember the tryouts? Well, you've proven to us that we made the right choice. You worked hard and you improved. We're really happy that you tried out and you are starting to think about the team on the ice." The kids' faces glowed and turned a bit pink as we complimented them. They were quick to look over at whichever parent was in the room to share their pride, and each of them left smiling.

None of it was a lie. They worked their tails off and every one of them improved. As far as I was concerned, we had already won this year. Many of the kids and parents took the opportunity to thank us for coaching. Greg told us about one parent: "Hey, one father isn't too happy. He walked by the other parents at the game last night and said we were out-coached again."

"Who cares?" said Steve. "It should only get to you if you let it."

One parent told us to "listen to the silent majority, not the louder minority." A number of parents remarked that their children had come out of their shell, gained confidence, and really enjoyed coming to the rink. Those were the most satisfying responses.

—ɯ—

Four more kids were down tonight and couldn't make practice: Missile, Ferrari, Swifto, and Ghost. Wheelsie is back after more than a week of the flu, but still not right. Today I scrimmage with Bartman and a few of the others.

"Hey, Mr. Arnold, I'm going to the Petes game tonight," yells Rocket. He's been sick for more than two weeks and is coming around. Wheelsie is all smiles to be back. I have a little game with Glovesy. When the action for our drills is at the other end of the ice, I take shots on him. If I score, he owes me a bubble gum. If he makes the save, I owe him one.

"You can buy them six to a pack, so two packs and we're even," he says after a while. Yes, I owe him twelve bubble gums. Remarkably, the kid thinks I have it in my pocket.

"Come on, Teak, where are the gums?" Sorry kid, you'll have to wait.

Jets has a sad story to tell me. "Hey, Eddie, I was at school today?" She often talks in questions. "And I was out playing at recess? And this kid, he fell on me? I've got a bruise on my leg." Then she skates away as fast as any kid that age could ever skate.

After practice Steve tells the kids he's going to Florida, "not to coach the Panthers," but on vacation with his family. He wishes them all luck. Greg will be out west for our next game, which will be played in a different arena from the one we usually play in. We have at least four kids sick. Everything is going our way.

In the dressing room Timbit takes off his helmet and, with obvious pride, he exposes his recently dyed hair of orange, yellow, and red.

"It looks like one of the boys got sick on your hair," I tell him. He doesn't disagree but says, "Pretty neat, eh?"

—⅏—

Johnny is here for the third game of the best-of-five – a home game against Whitby. We're down two games to none. The kids are pumped. Missile is here, but he's sick. Jonathan Nauta is here, but he's sick too. I tell them just to give everything they have, that's the best we can ask for . . . and they do.

We take an early 1–0 lead and we're all over them. Unfortunately for us, their goalie is playing awesomely. Gloves starts the game and kicks out several sensational shots as well, and stops one breakaway. It's a neat minor hockey game. Back and forth. It's 1–0 in the third and we run out of gas. Whitby scores three goals. We still have our chances but their goalie continues his hot streak. We always switch goalies in the middle of each game, and we do it again today. Whitby beats us 3–1.

Some kids are crying when they come off the ice. I tell them I'm proud of all of them. Although we lose this series 3–0 and Whitby goes on to the Ontario Minor Hockey Association semifinals, we now go on to our league championship. I tell the team this and, when they realize there is more hockey to be played, it picks them up.

Johnny has brought chocolate for every player. I feel badly for Missile and Ferrari. They are obviously still sick and very quiet.

I go to the Whitby dressing room, congratulate the team, and wish them well in the next round. We have seen Whitby improve with each game, each week of the season. And we can't overlook another joy of minor hockey – the happiness on those Whitby kids' faces.

—⚉—

"Hey, coach, how are things doing?" Steve is phoning from Florida. His family has been to see Disneyland and is enjoying the weather. I look outside. It's freezing rain. We talk about practices coming up (he loves practices). I am touched and amazed that he has taken the time to call, but, as his family says, "his mind's back in Peterborough with the team."

I asked Greg to run practice tonight. He's wearing an incredibly green helmet, a leftover from his days with the Hartford Whalers. He tries three-on-threes, passing drills, one-on-ones, and British Bulldog. Coppo is in Sudbury for the native hockey tournament. Missile is sick again with infected sinuses. The poor kid is on March break and not allowed to leave the house.

"It may not be good to use an excuse," says Greg, "but I really think if we were healthy we could have given the team a run."

"Hey, Eddie," says Jets. "I won Petes tickets."

"How?"

"I don't know." Okay.

The scrimmage before our practice starts has become physical between two of our players, Colin and Riley. I watch and don't stop it. They push and shove each other several times. When our practice starts, I get the two of them to go around the ice once with each other to remind them they are linemates and teammates.

Glovesy and I have our little bubble-gum game again today. I beat him this time – a first (I've already turned over two packs of gum in the last two weeks).

"Okay, you owe me a pack," I tell him.

"Uh, uh," he replies and agrees with me when I ask "What? Does it only count when *you* win?"

Practice goes fast. My feet are frozen. Parents are again asking me when the next playoffs begin. I don't know, it's in the hands of league schedulers. Once teams are out of the OMHA playoffs, the OMHA really doesn't focus much on the teams left to play for their league championships or, as some people call them, the kiss-your-sister round.

Greg is still trying to talk me into coaching next year. I look around at the kids and ask myself again: "Do I really have the heart to make tough decisions if I have to cut one or a few of them next year?"

—❧—

Practice. Ghost is trying his darndest to open the rink door to get off the ice. He looks frantic. I skate over.

"Where you going, Ghost?"

"Gotta go."

"Where you going?"

He looks up, red-faced. "I have to pee and I have to pee now." The door is opened and away he goes.

Coppo is back. He scored four goals in the Native tournament and was voted player with the biggest heart. I tell the team of his accomplishments. Coppo flashes that proud smile of his and the rest of us bang our sticks to congratulate him. Missile is still sick.

I'm letting Bill run practice today. Greg is here, but I want to see one of Bill's practices. If I don't come back next year, Bill may be the new coach. He runs excellent skating drills. We have a fast practice with plenty of skating, passing, and shooting.

Ghost comes back on the ice with a big look of relief on his face. Jets is spraying snow on me every chance she gets. Glovesy is looking for more gum.

I've been on the ice today since 3:25 p.m. I couldn't wait to get on the ice; at the newspaper we had a Hells Angels member visit this afternoon, Trent University is in an uproar over a student occupation, a man made some threats because we had his arrest printed in the paper, two reporters called in sick, I'm fighting a head cold. . . .

—∿—

Still no word on the next playoff round, and that's what's on every parent's lips again today. Steve is back from Florida looking tanned and relaxed. He's hoping we don't start the playoffs tomorrow night because his daughter Bailey's last hockey game of the season is tomorrow night. (I bet that's when our game will be.)

M. G., the Thrill, is sick today. He has strep throat. Bill still comes to practice. I told the team Steve was buying a home and jet in Florida. They asked him when they could fly on the jet.

"Ah, payback time, is it?" he asks.

The kids aren't focused on practice. No matter how much fun we make practice, you can tell they are just waiting to play a game. Missile is back. He's still not 100 per cent, but he's feeling much better.

Ghost is impressed. He gave me some Montreal Canadiens tape for my stick blade at the last practice and it's on my stick today. We had some shooting practices today. The kids owe me twelve gums.

I'm home by 6:30 tonight. The phone rings. It's the playoff scheduler. After twelve days without a game, we're going to start . . . tomorrow night. The game will be in Peterborough against Richmond Hill. Steve won't be there. Greg is in Phoenix. We're not sure if M. G. will be healthy, but Bill will be at the game. I have to telephone the parents to let them know. Richmond Hill will drive here on a school night for a 7:30 p.m. game. That's not fair, but the next series has to start next week. The season is winding down. While I think the coaches and adults will be glad when it's over, the kids are in no rush. They are in playoffs. It's like playing for the Stanley Cup or, as Swifto tells his older brother, Mike (whose team got beat out last weekend), "Hey, at least we're still playing."

—m—

Game day. Surprise, surprise: the kids start to pay me their gums. Gloves brought me a whole pack and Ferrari brought three gums. Hicksie owes me four and didn't bring any but yells out, "If we win are all debts off?" Good idea. That's a deal. Johnny shows up. Thrill is back and looks healthy.

This series will be a best-of-three, with the winner going to a round-robin format for the league championship. In the dressing room before the game I go over the options. Coppo has his hand up for a question. I give him a look. He takes down his hand and says, "Never mind, it's not a good question." I continue, but then I think better of it.

"Okay, Coppo what was it?"

"What are the lines?"

I continue. I tell them what the series is all about, how Richmond Hill would like to beat us in our own rink. Charlie's hand goes up. Now, this should be a good question, Gloves never sticks his hand up while I'm talking with the team.

"Yes, Glovesy."

"If we lose are we still going to have a party?" No! Just kidding.

Away we go. Johnny will be opening the door to change the forwards and obviously isn't used to it. We haven't had shifts this long since our Pickering tournament in September when Steve was giving three-minute shifts.

"You try and get them off the ice," Johnny says to me. I tell Wheelsie his shift was "the longest in the history of hockey." He just smiles. A few minutes later another line comes off, and I tell them that was far too long to be on the ice.

"Longer than mine?" asks Wheelsie.

Ghost has the puck in our own zone. Nobody is near him. If he takes off, he'll have wide-open ice. Everyone else is on a line change. Instead, he dumps it down the ice. As he comes off, he looks at me with a little smile and says, "Guess I could have gone with it, right?" I smile back and say, "Next time," knowing it's not likely to happen for a long time. Oh well, at least he'll be ready for the next time. Ghost has come a long way. He's our top shot-blocker. He loves doing that, which is very unusual in minor novice.

Gloves makes an astounding breakaway save. The play goes down to the other end of the ice. He looks over at me and I wave the pack of gum at him. We win the game 5–2. Jets scores a great goal. She breaks out at centre, beats the skates off a defenceman, and then scores, putting the puck between the goalie's legs. There are two seconds left in the game.

"Right in the five hole," she yells at me.

One line hasn't been passing much, and all three forwards have complained to me about the others not passing. I bring them together and get them to voice their concerns in front of each other. It doesn't work – one of them will have to pass to get the others doing it, too.

"I've been passing," says Missile, who did pass a couple of times. In the dressing room I congratulate everyone, but point out one line wasn't passing, and they know who they are.

"I was passing," says Missile again. As we hand out gum and licorice, we remind them of practice tomorrow. I'm leaving the rink when I run into Missile again.

"I was passing," he says.

"I know, Missile, I know."

The kids all look healthy. They played well. Everything is right in Peterborough land.

—⁓—

Greg calls today from Phoenix. Why? Just to tell me he was sitting by the pool and about to go golfing. Good. I'm sitting in my office looking out my window at snowbanks.

I beat Steve to the rink, only the third time at practice this year. We have a great conversation before the practice, just talking about life, something we don't get much time to do.

Jets has brought me two pieces of gum today. "I owe you them from the practice," she says. I thank her and later thank her father, Gene.

"Yeah, we had to stop and get them on the way to the rink. But she says she's going to get them back from you tonight and challenge you to a race," he warns me. We all know she would beat me.

"I could beat you in a race, Eddie," she says to me later, on the ice.

"You're not that fast, Jets," I reply.

"I could beat you, that's the thing," she says.

"I could beat you any time I want to," I say.

"Let's race," she says.

"I don't want to." She sprays me with some ice and away she skates.

Rocket isn't at practice tonight. We didn't get a phone call but one kid says he wasn't coming tonight "because he said he didn't have a reason." Interesting. I call him after practice and he says he "threw up at school."

Steve and I discuss the banquet awards. Each team in the minor Petes system has to pick the most dedicated, sportsman-like, and improved players. How do we do that with seventeen eight- and nine-year-olds who all try? It's too tough to call. We're going to have our own team banquet and give awards to all players.

I taunt Jets, showing her the two gums she gave me. She smiles calmly and says, "I could beat you in a race." I know you can, but you're not getting these gums back.

It's Ferrari's birthday today. He doesn't know I know. He's just going on the ice. "Ferrari, you look different today, so much older," I say.

"I am, I'm nine today," he says with a grin and shoots off onto the ice.

Steve says Bailey is interested in trying out for the girls' rep team next year. She's a goalie. He told her he might help coach the team if she makes it but she'd have to listen to him as a coach, not just as a father. Her reply? "Oh, Dad, what do you know about goalies?" We both laugh. She should look at the record books.

Overheard in our dressing room: "We could be playing longer than the Habs this year." No respect.

—m—

"That's what I want to be," says Gloves, his big brown eyes glued to the television screen on our bus as we make our way toward Richmond Hill for game two of the semifinals. The kids are watching a movie called *MVP*. It's a kids' show about hockey and a monkey.

"You want to be a hockey player?" I ask.

"No, a monkey." I break out laughing.

"No, seriously, Teak, I'd like to be a monkey," he says. I look at him. He sticks his upper lip in his mouth, pushes out his lower lip, pulls his ears to imitate a monkey. "Is this a true story?" he asks.

Gloves will also be the topic in the dressing room when we get to the rink. He has forgotten to pack his blocker and glove. He was playing mini hockey at home and forgot to put them back in his hockey bag. He and Thrill will share. Monkey, indeed.

—∞—

We don't start the game very well. We're scrambly and lethargic. Richmond Hill takes a 2–0 lead. We don't wake up until halfway through the game. One of our goals has Coppo leaping on the bench, right on Gloves, whose skate lands on my ankle.

At the beginning of the third period, our team is waiting for the faceoff. Richmond Hill's team is over at the bench. The ref tells me we have a two-minute break. I call our team over, but their team goes to the faceoff and the ref says we can start whenever we want.

"Okay, guys" is about all I get out. The ref drops the puck. Coppo skates past our bench and as he does, he shouts, "Nice speech, Mr. Arnold." We all break up, including the Richmond Hill coaches.

We come back and tie the game 3–3. This means we play another game tomorrow in Peterborough. If we lose, another game will be played. We need a win or tie tomorrow. It's a

penalty-free game today, our second of the season. In thirty-five
league and playoff games we've had ninety-two penalties, no
majors; the vast majority were for tripping.

Bailey and Bart's sister buy candy for all the kids after the
game with their own money. On the way home Steve calls Greg
in Phoenix and tells him about Charlie forgetting his glove and
blocker. He also tells him we had to buy a new set for $433
and the team would give him the bill tomorrow. Greg falls for
it hook, line, and sinker. "Maybe Play It Again Sports will buy
them, after all, it was only used for one game," he says. Steve cor-
rects him: "Half a game."

—w—

Ferrari says he has to score tonight because his mum said if he
did he could dye his hair maroon. He does score. When he gets
to the bench, he points to his mum in the crowd.

We also get a shutout, which means I owe the team another
pizza. They say I now owe them six. I tell Greg that Charlie wants
to be a monkey. Thrill overhears me and says "So, I want to be
a gorilla." We have a new "good-luck charm" brought to the team
by Wheelsie. It's a furry stuffed Irish leprechaun. It works for
him. He gets two goals.

It was one of the better games we've played. It helps that the
players have their health back. The Richmond Hill goalie was a
good one. We probably had a dozen great scoring chances.

The kids want me to give them another "speech" between
periods. They come over to the bench. Yesterday's was simply
"Okay, guys." Today they ask me to make it shorter so I just
say, "Go."

We win 6–0. We went from a penalty-free game yesterday to
six penalties today. That's minor hockey, you never know what
team will show up. Thrill and Gloves played great, as did the rest

of the team. Steve had them playing shorter shifts. The kids came off complaining about shorter shifts, but they had more energy, looked better, and were all making good decisions. Now we wait to see whom we play in the next round, the league championship round. It's a round robin against two other teams, a home-and-away series. That means four more games and two more bus trips. Yes, we probably will be playing longer than the Habs.

—⚏—

It wasn't until about halfway through today's practice I realized this was our last practice and the coaches weren't even on the ice. The Ontario Hockey League's Bantam Hockey Championship tournament (OHL Cup) is being held in Peterborough, and as part of the festivities a member of the Canadian Hockey Association will conduct clinics with our team and several others. A member is on the ice with our team today.

Steve, Greg, Bill, and I are watching it. We have our playoff schedule. We play Thursday, Friday, Saturday, and Sunday, then we're done. Today, as we watch, I feel robbed that we're not on the ice with our kids.

"How did you like that practice, Timbit?" I ask later.

"Better than anything you guys do," he retorts with a laugh. (We *think* we heard him laugh.)

During the drive home I realize the hockey stick I've had in my car between the front seats for the last seven months (the one my wife is always moving in frustration) will have no further use this season. The skates, cones, pucks, helmet, gloves in my trunk are no longer necessary. Steve will not have to put together any more practices. There will be no more meetings of the players and coaches on or off the ice.

Greg will be in Chicago Wednesday, back here for Thursday's game, and miss the rest of the games. We play at home

Thursday, then in Ajax Friday, in Barrie Saturday, and back at home Sunday.

Steve and I discuss awards again today. How, pray tell, do you pick three kids from this group of seventeen? It's not fair and the awards shouldn't exist. Every one of these kids has improved so much. Most are dedicated and sportsmanlike – "Nicole can't get sports*man*like, can she?" jokes Steve. Steve and I, the two non-parents, will make the selections. No pressure.

—⁂—

First game of the league championships round robin. Ajax–Pickering play us at home. The slogan for tonight's game? Four days left, four games left. The Ajax–Pickering team is delayed getting here because of an accident on Highway 401.

The team is excited about the finals. Kirk "Dinger" Bartley promises to score me a goal. Kirk has had several nicknames this year: Bartman, Batman, Barts, and now Dinger, his favourite. He got this name for dinging the puck off the crossbar in the last game. I had the kids put four strips of tape on their pants today to signify four games left, but the tape kept falling off, so we scrapped it after the warmups.

Ajax–Pickering came to play. They take a 2–0 lead. We fight back. The referees call back two of our goals. One referee came over to apologize after a goal.

"Sorry about that, the puck was in but I blew my whistle too quickly." Hey, we all make mistakes. A few years ago I would have been hollering and screaming at him.

"Don't worry, we'll get it back," I say. Within two minutes we do. The referee comes back to the bench and says, "I didn't think it would be that quick."

Dinger misses the crossbar and gets a goal. "Hey, you kept your promise, Batman," I tell him.

"Dinger, Mr. Arnold, Dinger." Oh, right. The game ends in a 3–3 tie. Why they don't have overtime is beyond me, but the adults set the rules.

It's hard to believe there are only three days, three games left.

—⟋ᴡᴧ⟍—

Road trip. We play in Ajax. Game time is 8:00 p.m. Steve and I have figured a way to get off the hook for the awards. I have the kids fill out their votes for Most Sportsmanlike Player, Most Dedicated Player, and Most Improved Player. During the trip I get the players to write their favourite memories of the year. Most of them picked their first goal, or hat trick, but some of them picked other things. Missile wrote, "The pass I made to Josh [Gregory] because it was his first goal and he was excited." For Triggerman, a.k.a. Nathan Larson, it was "when Riley was at the red line and he carried the puck into our end and went around our net." (I remember that so well. We thought he was going to shoot on our own net.) The goalies had different choices – Glovesy loved doing glove saves but the Thrill (Mitch Gillam) chose "Getting an assist in a game because goalies don't get to do it." The last word goes to Coppo, whose favourite memory was "Giving Mr. Arnold that fish that he ate in three gulps."

The Ajax coach welcomes us at the door. We win the game 3–2. Nice hosts.

—⟋ᴡᴧ⟍—

Game day. The last bus trip of the season. It was at the end of September that we made our first bus trip, and that, too, was to Barrie.

Steve and Bill went to a clinic run by the OMHA on abuse and harassment. Every coach and minor hockey official will have to take this clinic to be able to coach next season. Hockey is getting so bureaucratic. Although I've coached for eleven years (not consecutive), I have to take the coaching course again. I'll also have to take this clinic, if I want to coach again in minor hockey.

We're playing at the army base (CFB Borden) near Angus, about fifteen minutes from Barrie. I remember several weeks ago, when Coppo interrupted one of my little pre-game speeches in which I was telling them what they could do. He had shouted, "This isn't the army, Mr. Arnold." As we enter the base, tanks and army equipment are everywhere. "Hey, Coppo, we're in the army now," I shout to him. Our parents encounter a bit of military officiousness when they enter the rink. A rink employee becomes angry because one young child in the lobby is not holding her parent's hand. A sign states there should be no un-supervised children under twelve. The parents are right there within ten yards of the child. He threatens to have the parents removed. One parent asks if he has kids. He replies, "Yeah, but I've got a firm grip on them." The employee calls the military police and wants all the Peterborough parents removed from the rink. It's an unbelievable situation. The Barrie parents are upset, embarrassed, and apologetic. The police arrive and an officer tells the parents if a rink staff person is ordering them out, there's not much he can do, but he'll try to talk with him. Fortunately, the parents are allowed to stay, but they miss the first period.

We take a pounding in the game and lose 8–3. We were never really in it until the third period. Steve thinks our kids are tired, and Rocket certainly looks a bit slower than usual at the first of the game. I ask him about it after the first shift.

"I have a cough," he says, and gives me two little coughs. Later, in the second period, he sees me watching him and gives me two more little coughs. I'm laughing inside now. In the third period I say, "Well, I guess you won't want to go to McDonald's with a cough like that."

"Oh, it's all right now," he says, and never coughs again.

Barrie coach Abram is what we call a loud coach. He yells directions at all the kids: "Pass it! Shoot it! Stay high! Hustle! Get off the ice! Dump it!" His voice echoes through the rink. It's Steve's belief that the coach just doesn't know what he sounds like. He's the father of one of the players. (I've been down that road. You tend to lose sight of things when your own children are involved.) He seldom lets up, even when his team is ahead 7–3. They are a talented and hard-working team and could have beaten us without the yelling.

After the game, I try to keep a straight face as I say, "Okay, since we lost there will be no McDonald's." The kids groan.

"All right then, we'll have a team vote. Who says we should still go to McDonald's?" The noise is deafening.

10

THE LAST TRIP

This is the last time I'll be on the kids' bus heading for a less-than-an-hour hockey game, two hours away from home. I looked around the forty-eight-seat coach with the television units, comfortable seats, and darkened windows. The parents were in the back, chatting, playing cards, and maybe breaking some rules. I didn't want to know. The kids were all up front. Steve, Bill, and I were in the front seats as usual. I listened to the sounds and looked around at the faces of the children. They didn't know it, but I had decided I wouldn't be back next year.

For now, I wanted to soak it all up. The memories were deep. The noise, laughter, vomiting, headaches, colds, sniffles, yelling, jokes . . . the fun. Jets was joking around as usual. She caught my eye and gave that long wink of hers. Woody had the music going. C. P. had another new wet hairdo. Missile was playing Nintendo games. Triggerman, Timbit, and Thrill's eyes were glued to the movie (*Dunston Checks In*). Dinger watched the movie, then talked, then watched. Coppo and Rocket were eating (they eat like horses). Glovesy was smiling, but he was a bit ill today so he wasn't as lively as usual. Wheelsie wanted a different movie, a hockey video with fights, but I didn't want to promote hockey violence. Swifto was up and down on his seat, undecided whether he wanted to watch a movie. J. G. was playing a game. (His five-year-old sister, Drew, was on the bus with her stuffed toy, Freddy.) Hicksie was watching the movie. Ferrari had a bit of motion sickness. Ghost was up to something, but you never knew what.

Bill and Steve were talking about this morning's clinic. We also talked about whether parents should have to attend clinics on how to behave before their child is allowed to play hockey. Shouldn't parents already know how to behave?

After a stop for food, I visited the back for the first time this year. It wasn't as noisy at the back. Then I sat in the middle of the bus with the kids. That's the noisiest spot! Some kids were getting up and walking the aisle. We asked them to have a seat. Suddenly, Drew's little friend, Freddy, was lost. People were looking all over the bus for him. Steve was looking under seats, but Freddy couldn't be found. (When Drew's mum called McDonald's that night, the manager told her they had found Freddy, assured Drew the toy was helping them cook, and promised she would "tuck Freddy in that night and tell him a nice bedtime story." They sent him home by Purolator the next day – the family said they always knew "Freddy was born to ride.")

I reminded the players it was our last bus trip.

"Yeah, so it should be fun," Swifto said.

"Yeah, fun, but not wild," I replied.

The biggest joy of coaching kids is the kids. Every practice, every game, the pressure of life is lifted. That's why I can no longer understand why coaches are yelling and screaming. Oh, I used to do some of the same things when I was younger and had a child on the team. But when you're with the kids on the bench or on the ice, it should be fun. Why do so many coaches stand with their arms tightly folded and a look on their face that would break a mirror?

The other night, in the lobby of a rink, seven of us were standing around talking. Gary Baldwin, the referee, was asking Steve about the hockey season so far. "This is the most fun I've ever had in hockey," he replied. Gary and the four other people laughed nervously. Steve and I didn't. Steve heard the "yeah right" in their laughter. He stopped and assured them, "I'm serious. This is the most fun I've ever had in hockey."

He *was* serious. I understood it, but the other people were caught off guard. I hoped these kids and parents would have more fun in the hockey years ahead of them. I believe that as they grow older, they'll realize this was a very special year. I've had other special years coaching kids. In fact, all but one were enjoyable. But this was the most *fun* I've had in hockey.

I looked around the bus again and thought about the future of these kids. I started coaching sixteen years ago and many of the kids we coached then are now in university or college. Three play junior hockey in the OHL. If these kids are like those kids, this bunch is made up of future teachers, doctors, lawyers, truck drivers, construction workers, mechanics, and farmers.

Just as the bus entered Peterborough I heard Dinger's voice.

"Hey, Mr. Arnold," he shouted. He asked the same question he has asked me on almost every bus trip this year. "Hey, Mr. Arnold. What time is it?" I gave him the same answer that I have given every kid who has asked me that question over the years:

"The best time of your life, kid, the best time of your life. And don't you ever forget it."

—⏦—

The season will end at home. It will end abruptly. We will go our separate ways. There will be a team banquet and a minor Petes banquet. Things will never be the same. But first we had another last to attend to: our last game.

—⏦—

The next day the minor novice Petes played Barrie again, our fourth game in four nights.

"Whose puck is it?" I asked them one more time.

"The Petes' puck!" they shouted in unison.

It was an amazing game that ended in a 4–3 Barrie win. It had been exciting and the competitive juices had been flowing, but we stuck to our philosophy of not double-shifting, not using game strategy, and always allowing the kids to play their own game.

During the game the referee had come to our bench. He told me that the fans – there were more than a hundred at our game that night – and Barrie coaches were getting louder all the time. He appreciated the Peterborough bench and its no-abuse, no-yelling policy. He speculated that some day the parents would have to be put in a warm room during minor hockey games. But fans love to cheer and jeer, and parents are no different.

The dying moments of the game still play in my mind as clearly as they unfolded on that night. Wheelsie hit the goalpost and came to the bench crying. Missile and Superman both had breakaways. Timbit made an end-to-end rush. When the last whistle was blown, the team went to where their parents were standing and gave them a cheer, having dedicated the game to their parents, who paid all their costs during the season, stuck with them all the way, got them to all the practices and games, and spent seven months sharing their trials and tribulations.

This, like all the games we played, had its moments of drama. Charlie (Loops Jr.?) Millen had forgotten his glove and blocker again (his mother had made the fifteen-mile trip to get them before he started the second half of the game). After the game some kids had tears in their eyes. I told them how proud I was of them and reminded them that sometimes you lose games that you should win. Then I turned to the team and asked them: "What time is it?"

They shouted in unison: "The best time of our lives!" And maybe it was.

EPILOGUE

True to our word, we had a team banquet. We held it in the back of a local restaurant with all the kids and their parents there to enjoy it.

At the banquet, I presented the following trophies to the players:

- Glovesy Millen and Thrill Gillam: Most Valuable Players
- Ghost Braithwaite: Defensive Specialist Award
- J. G. Gregory: Best Dekes Award
- C. P. Curtis: Heads Up Player Award
- Hicksie Hickey: Versatile Player Award
- Triggerman Larson: Quick Release Award

- Timbit Baker: Most Aware Award
- Super Woodbeck: Strongest on Feet Award
- Jets Gifford: Most Determined Award
- Wheelsie Sharpe: Top Faceoff Award
- Rocket Rochon: Top Shot Award
- Dinger Bartley: Smartest Player Award
- Missile Donohoe: Stickhandler Award
- Swifto Swift: Grittiest Player Award
- Ferrari Nauta: Strongest Player Award
- Coppo Coppaway: Best Spirit Award
- John Lawson: Mr. Positive Award
- Katherine Sharpe: Best Organized Award

—◊◊◊—

The Esso Awards were given out at the minor Petes banquet:

Most Sportsmanlike: Jeff Braithwaite (three minor penalties all year, the least on the team besides Kirk, with one, but he got another award)

Most Dedicated Player(s): Nicole Gifford and Kirk Bartley

Most Improved: Michael Hickey (He asked his dad: "Does this mean I was the worst on the team at the first of the year?")

—◊◊◊—

The kids, all dressed in shirt and ties, brought the coaches gifts, cards, and an individual hockey card of them. I especially liked Nathan Larson's card. He designed it himself. It had a picture of a lonely hamburger and asked the question "Where are the fries? Oh yeah! Ed ate them." Then he added: "A couple more acts of kindness like those, and you'll join the lucky few I have on my speed-dial."

—◊◊◊—

York Simcoe defeated the undefeated Markham team at the OMHA finals but were defeated by the Halton Hurricanes in the championship game.

—∿—

Let's not forget the parents. They didn't get any awards (except for Katherine Sharpe, in her role as manager) but they were rewarded with lots of memories.

Many of them remembered firsts: "The first goal [Brad] got" (Sherri Baker); "The first time Ghost stepped on the ice with that Petes sweater on" (Andy Braithwaite); "Wesley's first goal I yelled, 'Oh my God, is that Wes?'" (Janice Coppaway); "[Stephen's] first game when he skated around with that uniform on and he got a hat trick" (Frank Woodbeck). For Dave Baker, who turned out to be a supportive hockey parent, it was a last: "Timbit's last rush of the season. I noticed he was opening up more and then he made that end-to-end rush in the last game of the year." Vicki Donohoe also had a "last" favourite memory: the last dinner the team had together. "I was so impressed that every player received an award and was recognized in such a positive way by the coaches."

Mike Bartley said, "I'd sooner watch those games than the big Petes, where all they do is dump and chase. There wasn't a time we couldn't have won if the philosophy had been different, but what's a minor novice championship compared with what they got?" Darlene Swift liked the way we congratulated the kids after every shift. She said, "Our older son saw this was happening all the time and said it had never happened to him."

Many parents mentioned the CBC program and what it had meant to them. Each of them had a special memory from the show. For Leslie Gifford, it was Nicole being the captain on the night of the taping. Michelle Gregory remembers "when

Jonathan Nauta got the hat trick and Johnny Lawson threw his hat onto the ice." Nathan Larson's mother, Annette, recalls, "We roared when we watched the CBC program. When we heard Steve [Larmer] and Jonathan joking around it was cute. We thought you were over there always talking about hockey." Karen Rochon is with these parents in mentioning the show as her favourite memory. She says, "I was on the bed and started jumping up and down. Riley told me to get a grip. I told him that was probably his moment of fame."

Janice Coppaway and Vicki Donohoe both mentioned the Santa Claus parade and its preparations.

And other parents have memories particular to their own children. Leslie Gifford recalls with fondness Nicole "sleeping over at Colin's and Kirk's and being accepted so well by the city kids." Ann Millen will never forget "the number of times Charlie forgot things." Cathy Perry mentioned Curtis's "dos." "He had to do his hair for Larms. He had to do the 'do' right or do it over." Speaking as a true hockey aficionado Gord Sharpe said, "My favourite game was when we lost to York Simcoe 3–0. We played hard and later beat them."

Paul Donohoe proudly cites the Barrie tournament as one of his best memories. "As a group all of us came together. That last game in the tournament against York Simcoe when we were down 2–0. Ryan got one goal and the crowd was still into it. Then, with twenty-three seconds left, he got another." Lloyd Rochon seconds this choice, using almost exactly the same words: "The Barrie tournament, when all they learned really came together."

Several parents mentioned enjoying watching the practices and Lloyd Rochon added that Riley loved them. A couple of parents singled out the bus rides (although the Perrys mentioned them specifically as not being a favourite memory at all!).

Greg Millen has a slightly different take on the bus rides, saying, "As much as I was dreading the bus trips, it brought us back to the grassroots of hockey that you lose at times – the smiles, the positive things, the fun and the honest passion you can see in these kids."

We weren't looking only for praise and positive comments. We questioned the parents on what their disappointments and criticisms were. Dave Baker thought "maybe AAA is a little too structured. Many coaches feel they are behind the bench so they are important. The question is, at what age do you coach the game and what age do you let them go?"

Our approach came in for some muted criticism. Paul Donohoe admits, "It was sometimes tough with the philosophy. It was new for everyone. I know Ryan respected it, but you'd go to the games and see the other teams win at all costs and it was tough to watch. The kids did well considering they had no set plays." Todd Gregory added to this, "I'd like to see more organization on the ice. It was tough to watch five guys go after the puck in front of our own net." Lloyd Rochon liked the philosophy but says, "It should have been universal in the league. We felt like a test centre. It should have been mandatory for every team." The Perrys had mixed feelings about the practice of the kids playing other positions. They say, "It was good, but it was difficult to watch when the kids weren't comfortable in new positions." But, they say, "All teams should do what you guys did. I didn't agree with some teams playing some players 75 per cent of the game."

Not surprisingly, several parents mentioned their counterparts on opposing teams as among the negative memories they took away. For Andy and Karen Braithwaite, it was the intensity of parents. Vicki Donohoe singled out "other parents from opposing teams yelling at the kids to take Ryan out." The Gillams complained about "some parents screaming at the kids telling them what to do, getting very wild. Our rule to have parents stand on the other side of the rink was a good one so parents can't as easily get the attention of their kids. Parents need to be cheerleaders." The Larsons said, "Parents yelling at refs, that's so embarrassing. We tell our children, 'Our team is going to make more mistakes than that referee – rise above bad referees.'" Speaking of the other teams' parents, the Nautas said, "Some other [parents] were bitter against us because of Steve and Greg coaching. It seemed to change after the CBC show and the parents heard about the team philosophy." Kathy Rochon had a muted objection to "one parent always calling it 'pond hockey,'" but she's quick to add, "Parents on our team were great but the yelling rule really helped. Riley would hear other parents but I told him to just ignore it." We were especially pleased with Frank Woodbeck's comments: "You hear horror stories and you don't believe it, but then we saw it when we went to other towns. Because of the team philosophy, we weren't as bad. I'm loud and cheer loud, but I couldn't believe what I heard. The team philosophy has actually had a calming effect on me when I coach [soccer]. I learned from you guys." Julie, Frank's wife, adds, "I must admit, when I saw the other teams playing their positions and going up and down their wings and they were shortening their benches, my competitiveness got the better of me sometimes."

Coaches didn't escape criticism, either. Michelle Gregory said, "I don't like to see coaches reaming the team out and losing control on the bench." The Hickeys agreed. They didn't like "the other teams' coaches yelling at the kids. Michael would ask, 'Why are those coaches yelling at them?' We don't talk to our kids that way and we wouldn't let others talk to them that way. We didn't like parents yelling at referees, either." Gord Sharpe believes, "Some parents aren't educated about hockey. My big beef has been that kids only get to play one position, but this year was great. I don't think parents are as bad as they used to be, but the coaches might be worse." Mike and Darlene Swift didn't like "coaches shortening the bench, playing favourites. We felt bad for some kids on other teams. If kids lose confidence they won't play the game."

The referees came in for some criticism too. Greg Perry said, "I know hockey is losing referees but unqualified refs are hurting hockey." His wife, Cathy, added, "I think refs at all age groups should be adults."

And finally, there were the hardships that being the parent or coach can bring. Nathan Larson's parents said, "We have no life, that's the hardest thing. Hockey becomes your life." Julie Woodbeck mentioned the "huge time commitment. When the season was over, we were ready." But probably no one felt the pressures of time, though from a slightly different perspective, more than Greg Millen, and more wistfully when he said the hardest thing was "being somewhere else when I'd rather be with the team."

What of the future? What do these hockey parents wish for their youngsters in the future? Almost unanimously, they wanted their children to benefit from higher education, and many saw hockey as their way to get that. Nicole Gifford's parents would like to see her play on a women's university team.

What about the kids? Bradley Baker wants to play against his brother in the NHL. Nathan Larson, Jeffrey Swift, Curtis Perry, and Kirk Bartley want to play in the NHL, Kirk specifically for the Leafs. Michael Hickey's ambitions are clear. His parents say, "He keeps asking if the Stanley Cup doesn't fit in his bedroom, where will he put it?" Cars seem to be a big motivator with these kids. Ryan Donohoe's dream is to play in the NHL and he tells his parents "Don't worry, I'll buy a car for you." Riley Rochon would love to play in the NHL so he could buy his mother a Honda so she'd be safer. Jonathan Nauta's dream is also to play in the NHL, buy his sister a yellow convertible and himself a green Ferrari to "give Mr. Arnold a ride in."

—◇◇◇—

After our season was over, Johnny Lawson became Don Cherry's trainer for the OHA Junior A Mississauga Ice Dogs, so the minor novice Petes already have someone who made it to junior hockey.

Bill Gillam became coach of the major novice Petes (Greg joined him after the tryouts, as did Frank Woodbeck and a non-parent, J. R. McGee). Thirty-three kids came out for the tryouts, three of them girls. Nicole's parents thought she would be thrilled if another girl made the team but when asked about it she said, "I don't want them messin' with my boys."

All of last year's kids tried out for the Petes the next year. Although Ghost didn't show up for the first tryout, he was there for the next one. Coppo, C. P., and Timbit didn't make the team this year, leaving three sad kids, but three happy ones who made it in their places. Coppo, C. P., and Timbit played for other local teams. They know there is always next year.

Colin Sharpe, because he was a year younger, had to stay with the minor novice team for another year and was far and away the best player on the Peterborough team.

Kirk Bartley saw me at a local golf course and gave me something he found in a pond. It was a golf ball with the Montreal Canadiens logo on it. "I don't want it. I'm a Leafs fan," he said, running away giggling.

I took a year off coaching to write this book, but went over to watch the team whenever I could. I miss them more than I thought possible.

Steve Larmer's role at the NHLPA was expanded, giving him less time to coach. Greg, Steve, and I spoke to the annual meeting of the Ontario Minor Hockey Association's coaching, trainer, and referee technical advisors about our experiences. Both Steve and I are interested in coaching again but also realize we may have just had the perfect season – a difficult thing to repeat.

APPENDIX A

Team Stats

	Goals	Assists	Points	Penalty Minutes
Bradley Baker	1	12	13	8
Kirk Bartley	30	19	49	2
Jeff Braithwaite	1	5	6	6
Wesley Coppaway	1	4	5	58
Ryan Donohoe	30	16	46	30
Nicole Gifford	8	17	25	12
Josh Gregory	12	17	29	22
Michael Hickey	1	9	10	20
Nathan Larson	10	9	19	6
Jonathan Nauta	9	9	18	42
Curtis Perry	1	9	10	16
Riley Rochon	17	17	34	6
Colin Sharpe	17	19	36	12
Jeffrey Swift	3	5	8	8
Stephen Woodbeck	28	13	41	26

APPENDIX B

Finances

The budget for the minor novice Petes 2000–2001

Total expenses:	$19,082.85
Total revenue:	$21,867
Bus expenses:	$6,728
Practice time:	$6,130
Two tournament fees:	$1,425.

Other expenses included such things as team photos, pizzas, and power-skating lessons.

Each parent paid $125 per month, as well as the registration fees, which totalled $5,500. The rest of the revenue came from fundraising. The parents raised $7,992 through their hockey pool, selling books, selling chips, having a tag day, and putting on bingos.

With more revenue than expenses, the parents all got money returned to them. The total cost of the year (excluding equipment, skate sharpening, gasoline, tournament expenses, etc.) for the child to play was $652 or $93 per month.

APPENDIX C

The Coaches' Philosophy

Before the children tried out for the team, the parents were given the following document, which outlined our philosophy. Surprisingly, this doesn't happen much in minor hockey. Usually the parents show up, pay their money for the ice time, watch the tryout, and listen to a stranger tell them their kid did or didn't make the team. Some coaches just tell the kid he doesn't have to come back, while others put a list on a door. The parents don't know until after the tryouts what the season will involve. We decided to communicate with the parents *before* the tryouts so they knew exactly what we were about – and what they were about to get themselves into.

> Tryouts for anything, whether it is a job, school or all-star sport can be a nerve-wracking experience. If the child doesn't make the team, it doesn't mean he or she is not a hockey player. It only means this year's coaches had to make difficult decisions to form the team.
>
> Peterborough and area have many different hockey organizations, and luckily, the children have many teams on which they can play. The Peterborough minor Petes AAA hockey system has a team from minor novice to midget in which players from the City of Peterborough and the

County can try out. If the child does not make this team, he can try out for the AA team if he's from Peterborough. If not, they go to their town or township team and play for their all-star teams. If they don't make an all-star team there are plenty of house-league teams.

The decisions coaches make at tryout time are the most difficult of the season. One important thing we tell parents is that AAA hockey means time commitment. We have at least two practices per week, two games per week, and plan to be in two tournaments (only one of which will be an overnight one, in January). The other is in September, before the season starts. We require the players to be at all of these. While many teams participate in overnight Christmas tournaments, we don't. However, we will have some scheduled practices over the Christmas holidays.

Tournaments are pleasant but the money is better spent practising. There will be plenty of tournaments later in life. Some of the best tournaments are at Christmas but Christmas is a family time.

Parents have to get their children to the practices to be on the ice when practice starts and have to be at the rink at least an hour before game time.

All of our players travel on a bus to and from the away games. This is not only a team rule but a minor Petes council rule started for the children's safety. The Council strictly enforces this.

Parents have to schedule holidays, and other dates, around the hockey team. The tournaments usually have games scheduled on Fridays, so the child may have to take time off school.

Cost is always an important factor when considering whether your child should play at this level of hockey. The estimated cost for the season is $130 per month. This pays for ice, some team equipment, coaches' development fees, tournament entry fees, buses, practice jerseys, pucks, cones, and other costs. There is also fundraising to participate in. The manager forms a fundraising committee. There is also a minor Petes council registration fee of $300 that will have to be paid after the tryouts.

The Minor Petes also expect parents to share door duty, where money is collected to pay for the referees, ice, insurance, etc., for the games.

A team manager is responsible for the revenues and expenses of the team: ice time, tournament costs, buses, and team equipment are the priorities of this budget. There will be a monthly statement issued by the manager.

We also told the parents we use only one thing to discipline our players: ice time. If the child misbehaves on the buses, at practice, or during the games, his ice time will be shortened as a form of discipline. Failure to make practices and tardiness may also have the same results; skating laps around the ice is sometimes used. If there is a more serious problem it will be addressed with parent(s). Failure to wear proper attire to the home and away games will mean he won't be allowed to participate. The council has a dress code for the players: shirts, tie, slacks, dress shoes to all games. He/she must wear a white helmet, maroon gloves and pants during games. The council supplies sweaters and socks.

Other matters we informed the parents of:

- The parent is responsible for getting the child to practice. The penalty for not attending practice is served by the child.

- No parents or other relatives are allowed at ice level during practices because it is a distraction for the players.
- We expect good behaviour on and off the ice.
- Parents should take up any problems directly with the coach. However, the coaches do not wish to hear complaints about positions, ice time, game strategy, and, most certainly, we do not wish to hear comparisons with other players.
- While "parent coaching" may be helpful, it sometimes is not in line with the coach's philosophy; you may be telling your child one thing while the coach wants him to be doing another. This can be a serious problem in AAA hockey and can interfere with the player and team development, creating confusion within the child.

We added:

The league is quite competitive and teams in other areas are quite good. There are creative juices flowing through some of these children, and, while there are times to pass and dump the puck, or play positional hockey, we also believe they should get back to stickhandling, deking, and using creativity.

Our practices will not just be repetitive drills. Although repetition is needed in such things as skating, we want to make practice competitive, fun, and hard work without the kids knowing how hard the practice is.

We want to win, but we're determined to do it with seventeen players.

The most important question is: does the child want to participate at this level of hockey?

We talked with each player and parent following the second tryout when we made our first tough decisions, and after every tryout following that. We didn't want to make tryouts a drawn-out affair but we did intend to give each child a fair chance.

We concluded our letter to the parents this way: "Remember: more than two billion people in the world don't care about hockey. No matter where your child plays the game, let it be their passion, not your obsession . . . and let these kids have fun.

"We wish your child all the best, if not this year at AAA level, then wherever he plays the best game in the world."

APPENDIX D

Recommendations

Here are some recommendations for minor hockey coaches:

1. Make sure all parents are aware of your rules, philosophy, commitment, and costs, *before tryouts*. An all-star team's most important decisions are at the tryout time. This is when you pick the players you'll be with all year. Pick the best players, who are usually the best skaters at an early age. Try not to have parents help pick the team. If you make the decisions based on talent, you'll feel far better for it.

2. Have safe and fun practices. Make sure the kids want to come for practice. Start it with a fun game, end it with a fun game. The Canadian Hockey Association has many valuable tips on practices.

3. Have a good coaching staff with the same philosophy.

4. Measure or set a benchmark at your first practice. Time the kids on certain drills, record their times, and then measure them again halfway through the year and at the end of the year on the same drills. This is important because it will tell everyone whether the children have improved. Wins and losses should not be the measurement of improvement at this age level.

5. Conduct one-on-one interviews with parents and children to discuss the benchmarks.

6. Have more practices, but fewer games and tournaments.

7. Put more emphasis on individual skills than on team strategy.

8. Let the kids make their own decisions on the ice. Give them options.

9. Let them be creative. Don't criticize them for trying something, just ask them if they had other options.

10. Allow them freedom.

11. Don't yell and shout at kids during a game.

12. Don't put pressure on them to win.

13. Emphasize sportsmanship; fair, clean play; and respect.

14. Make sure the skills you are teaching are age-specific.

15. Remember: all the parents are paying the same amount for their child to play, so give them fair ice time.

16. If you, the coach, are not laughing at practice or games, you may be in the wrong place.

17. Treat the kids with respect.

18. Let them all take turns as captains and assistants (goalies aren't allowed to be under the rules).

19. Avoid out-of-town Christmas tournaments for the early age groups. Let the kids enjoy Christmas with their families.

20. Give them all a chance to play wing, centre, and defence.

21. Coach them all, not just the most talented.

22. Leave them with positive reinforcement after games and practices.

23. Get rid of those long road trips for kids. Form leagues closer to home.

AFTERWORD

The 2000–2001 season was the best year in hockey that I have had. I played on the Stanley Cup team in 1994 with the Rangers and on a Canada Cup–winning team in 1991. This year in minor hockey was just as rewarding. It was fun. We let the kids play the game as they saw it and make their own decisions on the ice.

It was incredible to see their growth, through self-discovery from the start of the season right through to the end.

I was able to participate in the Molson Open Ice Summit in 2000 and two things said there have stuck with me. On the first day Bob Gainey asked, "Is it our job to produce players to play in the NHL or is it to provide a safe and fun environment for our kids to learn and grow?"

Janet Starkes, a professor of kinesiology at McMaster University, commented that what made Wayne Gretzky such a great player – his ability to anticipate and to be creative with the puck – is teachable. Wayne was always thinking three steps ahead of everyone else.

I would ask myself these questions every day at the rink. I think we have a responsibility as coaches to provide a safe and fun environment for our children to play in. We also have a responsibility to pay attention to all of the kids, not just the best ones. We wanted all of our kids to play in all situations and they did: power-play, penalty-killing, first-minute, and last-minute. They all excelled in these situations. We wanted them to carry the puck, beat players one-on-one, skate with speed, move the puck to the open player. We wanted them to take chances – no risk, no reward – to find out for themselves what they were capable of rather than us telling them what they could and could not do. We wanted them to play with confidence, knowing that if they made a mistake they were not going to be benched for it. We wanted them to think outside the box rather than inside the box. We wanted them to make their own decisions, with and without the puck, rather than us always telling them exactly what to do.

We had a great year, and all of our coaches were on the same page. Ed, Greg, Bill, and Johnny were all very positive both during practice and in the games. We were constantly talking about the philosophy we wanted to implement. We wanted our players to be as excited about practices as they were about playing the games. We wanted our players to play with the attitude I Can, I Can, rather than I Can't.

Coaches have to set the example. In all my years of playing hockey, I have found the team will take on the coach's personality. If you have an aggressive coach you will have an aggressive team, if you have a vocal coach you will have a vocal team. If the coach starts yelling at the ref then his players will start yelling at the ref. When we stop focusing on the game, the players will too. We have come to depend on the refs to control the behaviour of the kids playing the game when, in fact, it is the coach's responsibility. We are the ones that define proper behaviour during games and, more importantly, during practice. The kids are always pushing the limit and it is up to us to teach them sportsmanship. Unfortunately, the word sportsmanship has not been associated with hockey for a long time.

We went through the full season and never complained once about a call. We congratulated the refs after every game. We should thank them for the job they do. As our kids are learning the game so are the refs. As our kids make mistakes so will the refs.

As for Janet Starkes's comment about being able to develop the creative side of the game, I don't know that you can teach it, but I sure think we have robbed our kids of the opportunity to discover those possibilities for themselves. I wanted to coach minor hockey because the coaches I played for made the game fun. I wanted to see the fun put back into the game because, if it is not fun, why would you want to do it? We wanted these kids to make some discoveries on their own. Sometimes we overcoach our kids, our expectations are too high. We can't teach Grade 12 math to Grade 2 pupils. We have to spend more time developing individual skills: skating, shooting, and passing instead of team systems that are taught at the expense of skill.

If you can't skate you can't play this game. Everything in hockey revolves around skating and balance. We spent our whole year doing balance drills, skating, passing, and shooting drills. We ended every practice with a game of some sort. We played a lot of three-on-three cross-ice so all the kids had to touch the puck. There is no place to hide in three-on-three. We wanted our defence to beat the first checker rather than just get rid of the puck. We wanted our forwards, once they got the puck, to either skate with it or move it to someone who was skating. We wanted our goalies to play the puck, come out and set it up for the defencemen, or move it up to the forwards. Our goalies often wandered from the net. We wanted them to make their own decisions as to whether they should or shouldn't. At the end of the year they were making better decisions and they were making them quicker. That is where I saw their greatest improvement; doing the little things right.

One parent asked me when we were going to work on positioning. My reply was, "they all seem to be standing in the right place when there is a faceoff; after the puck is dropped they have to figure out where to go." The parent was surprised but these kids were capable of figuring out a lot on their own. They communicated well with each other. They supported each other well, both with and without the puck. They discovered a lot about themselves as hockey players and as individuals.

Not once during the year, neither in tournaments nor playoffs, did we shorten the bench or have specific power plays and penalty killers. We were beaten by teams that gave more ice time to their best players, and played their best goalie. Were we beaten by a better team or were we beaten because an adult made a decision to win with his best players and sit his weaker players? How much fun is it for the child who sits on the bench? How will we know what that child is capable of doing?

I think we, as adults, control the game way too much. We should have a definitive season, start tryouts a week after Labour Day and end the season at the end of March. There is an unnecessary overlap in seasons with hockey and the summer sports. Hockey should not compete with soccer, baseball, and lacrosse. We should be encouraging our kids to play different sports.

Without meaning to, we put pressure on our kids to commit either to winter or summer sports. The people who run these sports should get together and define their seasons so the kids can play what they want. There could even be some downtime between them so the kids could get some rest.

Are our coaches using the kids to promote their own careers or are they there to help all of the kids all of the time? Are our coaches buckling to the pressure of parents who demand winning teams, because they imagine that their son will play in the NHL? The good players will make it no matter what. We have a responsibility to the 99 per cent who won't.

— STEVE LARMER

ACKNOWLEDGEMENTS

I have learned many things, and made mistakes, about minor hockey after being a hockey parent, coach, trainer, and manager of various teams. I have learned from some wonderful coaches I coached with. In fact, they all had great ideas and coached for the right reasons. I am lucky to have worked with them and I thank them. I like to think I took some of their best ideas, mixed them with ours, and used them during this season.

Steve Larmer and Greg Millen encouraged me to write this book and get it published. They believe it may help other parents, coaches, and hockey officials. I thank them, not only for all they have done, but for their love of the game, the children, and their willingness to "walk the walk."

Canadian writer Roy MacGregor encouraged me to finish this project. His support was enough to keep me going. It's amazing that a telephone call from someone who also cares about children's hockey can be so encouraging. It meant so much to me for him to take the time and show such interest. Another author and a Canadian hockey icon, Dick Irvin, also encouraged me. I count myself lucky to have their support.

The Peterborough Examiner, my working home for more than thirty years, has always been supportive. Another hockey parent, Terry Keating, a fellow *Examiner* employee, has been through the rigours of minor hockey and encouraged me to write this book all along the way. The poor guy had to listen to my thoughts on every jog. But, we had finally found something to agree about.

Bob Gainey, a Peterborough boy who made it big in professional hockey, took the time to support the book. I am indebted to him and will pay the debt back on a Stoney Lake summer weekend.

There are so many others to thank. People whom I have not even met but whose writing about hockey has helped me become a better coach. William Houston's excellent series, "Game in Crisis," in the *Globe and Mail*, was one example. The writings of Rick Wolff, Steve Simmonds, Gary Mason, Ken Dryden, and Scott Young (I grew up reading his hockey books for young people), and other reports in newspapers and magazines across Canada that care about minor hockey, were invaluable.

The CBC's *Hockey Night in Canada* crew included our team in a 2001 documentary. The crew showed a genuine interest in our philosophy and the children. The children will always have a memory on tape thanks to the CBC. There were so many wonderful people willing to share their time such as Bill Schipilow of Dartmouth, Nova Scotia, who cared enough to change a system he found lacking in some areas. Johnny Misley and Brad Pascall of the Canadian Hockey Association, hoping to improve the game for all the kids who play it, were helpful in tracking down information. I thank Jim Parcells for his amazing statistics. I thank the coaches in the league who took the time to talk with me as well as the referees, especially Gary Baldwin.

Peterborough is a city with a hockey community that cares about children. I've been so lucky to have met and worked with so many of those people.

While I had these people to encourage the project, none of it could have been accomplished without the vision of Jonathan Webb and Doug Gibson of McClelland & Stewart. They believed in this book because they also believe it may help Canada's game. I am also grateful to Adam Levin at M&S for his attentive copyediting.

I thank editor Wendy Thomas. She was wonderful to work with. I knew we were on the same track when she said she had fallen for the kids and would really miss them.

This is the story of one season with a minor novice hockey team. A very special group of kids and parents. I wish them all good health in whatever their pursuits and thank them for their special efforts.